SCAM!

PETER H. ENGEL

SCAM

DISCARD

$\mathcal{S}$HAMS, $\mathcal{S}$TINGS, AND $\mathcal{S}$HADY $\mathcal{B}$USINESS $\mathcal{P}$RACTICES, AND HOW YOU CAN AVOID THEM

$\mathcal{S}$T. $\mathcal{M}$ARTIN'S $\mathcal{G}$RIFFIN 🐾 NEW YORK

Another book by
AFFINITY COMMUNICATIONS CORP.

Many of the names and details in this book have been fictionalized.

A THOMAS DUNNE BOOK.
An imprint of St. Martin's Press.

DESIGN BY SONGHEE KIM

Library of Congress Cataloging-in-Publication Data
Engel, Peter H.
    Scam! :   shams, stings, and shady business practices, and how you can avoid them / by Peter H. Engel.
        p.   cm.
    ISBN 0-312-14409-1
    1. Fraud—United States—Prevention.   2. Deceptive advertising—United States.   3. Business enterprises—Corrupt practices—United States.   4. Consumer education—United States.   I. Title.
HV6695.E54   1996
364.1'63—dc20   96-18
                                                                                    CIP

First St. Martin's Griffin Edition: May 1996

10   9   8   7   6   5   4   3   2   1

CONTENTS

CONTENTS

3

Senior Citizen Scams 16

4

Travel Trickery 24

5

Don't Be a Chump for Charity 36

6

*A*UTOMOBILE *S*CAMS **44**

7

*T*AKING *C*HANCES—*C*ONTESTS, *S*ALES, AND *P*ROMOTIONS **56**

8

*T*ELEPHONE *T*REACHERY **63**

CONTENTS

CONTENTS

12
SHOW BUSINESS SCAMS 95

13
SCAMS ON THE INTERNET 106

14
STAIRWAYS TO HEAVEN: RELIGIOUS AND "IMMORTALITY" SCAMS 111

15
INFOMERCIALS 117

16
SINGLES SCAMS 121

CONTENTS

17

PᴇᴛSᴄᴀᴍs 128

x

ACKNOWLEDGMENTS

*I*n Hollywood, it seems that even the hairdresser's husband gets a thank-you on Oscar night. While books are a far less communal venture than films, those who work "behind the scenes" are an essential part of the process.

Many thanks to Beverly Trainer for her editorial and creative contributions. And to Howard Cohl, vice president of Affinity Communications Corp., thank you for your insights and professionalism. Kudos also to Karen Grube for her meticulous copyediting and to Dean Harris for his impressive research.

INTRODUCTION

Most of us don't think much about scams unless we come across an item in the paper, usually a headline involving some multimillion-dollar swindle. We seldom realize that scams are ubiquitous and come in a variety of forms. Many of them are actually legal, just within the bounds of the law, and they intrude into literally every part of our lives.

"Legitimate" scams may involve ads that make skillful use of misleading words and phrases and ambiguous claims such as "our product is better." Better than what? The old axiom "Read the fine print" has never been more relevant, as labels, contest rules, and advertisements are increasingly created with deception in mind.

While snake-oil salesmen in the horse-and-buggy days had to rely on signs, posters, and their gift of gab, today's hi-tech world offers scam artists new windows of almost limitless opportunity. Telephone 900 numbers frequently offer services or information that is either a full-fledged or borderline rip-off. And computer on-line scams can literally reach millions in minutes. As much as we benefit from the convenience of technological advances, we've also become vulnerable to scam artists who can now access us with a touch of the dial or computer keyboard. We don't even have to venture out of our homes in order to become a target.

There's the old saying, "You can't cheat an honest man." Although many scams appeal to the victim's desire to "get something for nothing," some of the cruelest and slickest operations are aimed at the bereaved, the old, the lonely, the ill, and the hopeless.

Some scams have tragic consequences, while others are merely annoying. But one thing is certain. Scams exist in literally every facet of life, and even the most isolated persons cannot avoid them. But forewarned, as they say, is forearmed. As you read *Scam!* you'll recognize some familiar rip-offs and be surprised by others. In some instances you may identify with the victim or be reminded of someone you know. But most of all you'll learn how to avoid the clever traps laid by hustlers, and you'll find out how to outsmart the outlaws.

SCAM

1
Food
and
Fitness
Scams

Back in the "bad old days," consumers and food manufacturers alike were concerned with only one thing, taste. Foods that were satisfying and considered "taste treats" were the products that ended up in America's shopping carts.

But along came our nationally raised health consciousness, and food marketing became a whole new ball game. While cholesterol counts and fat grams used to matter only to health nuts, most mainstream consumers now shop with at least one eye on calories, cholesterol, and fat. Even hard-core grease eaters can no longer gulp down a cheeseburger without a chaser of guilt.

This collective food conscience is being catered to by food manufacturers of all types, from cereal makers to fast-food barons. The problem is that consumers want to have their cake without remorse. And this, of course, creates the temptation for packagers to (no pun intended) fudge a bit on their labels.

Because false advertising is prohibited by law, "snake-oil medicine" and other blatant hypes are outlawed on Madison Avenue. Ah, but what creative minds can do with those gray areas! No manufacturer would dare state that its veggie burgers will cure cancer (or any other specific ailment), but there's nothing to stop it from implying that its product is beneficial in the broader sense.

The Fine Print

Because truly fat-free-cholesterol-free-sugar-free foods are often reminiscent of recycled cardboard, no right-thinking entrepreneur can afford to package food that is healthful but tasteless. For many companies the solution seems to be a compromise: a not-so-healthful dollop of taste wrapped prettily in a label that's good for the soul.

A prime example of shading the truth is often found on the front of breakfast cereal cartons. The word "granola" has become nearly synonymous with healthful eating, as in "I used to eat bacon and eggs for breakfast, but now I just have a bowl of granola and a glass of juice."

But wait a minute! Many of these crunchy-nutty grains owe their "goodness" to sugar and fat. Some are loaded with coconut oil, a vegetable oil as high in cholesterol as most animal fats. While cereal boxes often proclaim in bold letters that the ingredients are "All Natural" or use "Only the Purest Honey," keep in mind that your pancreas doesn't know the difference between sugar and honey. All sugars, whether raw or refined, undergo the same process of metabolization.

So what may seem like a guilt-free way to break the fast may actually be a land mine of fat and sweets. I'm not suggesting that you start your day with eggs and doughnuts (although such a meal might contain fewer calories than some granolas), but if you're serious about your health, reading the fine print is a must.

While the big type might shout "All Natural!" or "Pure Vegetable Oil!" the fine print on the back of a package may own up to significant grams of both fat and cholesterol. Even when the truth is told, weight-conscious nibblers need to beware and be knowledgeable. Mono- and polyunsaturated fats (such as olive and safflower oils) are certainly cholesterol free, but they consist of no protein and no carbohydrates, just pure

2

fat. And one heart-healthy tablespoon contains no fewer than 15 fat grams and around a 100 calories. Use a generous helping on your salad and, calorie and fatwise, you might as well be downing a hamburger.

So what's the answer?

Reading the fine print on food labels is just a matter of habit. Once you get the hang of it you'll know exactly where to look, and it will soon become automatic. Think of it this way: The few seconds it takes to check out a manufacturer's claims will save you countless amounts of calories, cholesterol, and fat grams over your lifetime. And that adds up to a whole lot of pounds! In the long run those few seconds you spend scanning a label will save you grueling hours on the treadmill trying to undo the damage caused by tricky and less-than-truthful slogans.

Here are a few commonsense rules of thumb:

- *Fat free* means that a food contains 0 grams of fat. This doesn't mean *calorie* free, though. So-called fat-free cookies may have as many calories as regular cookies.
- *Reduced fat, fewer calories, lite, cholesterol free, no saturated fats,* and *all natural* are all euphemisms. Fat grams in such an item may range from 1 or 2 to zillions. Check the count on the back of the package.

For example, a product could be "97% fat free" yet still have 30, 40, or even 50 percent of its total calories derived from fat. Theoretically, something could even be 99 percent fat free and yet contain 100 percent fat calories. How is that possible? Simple: Mix 99 grams of water with 1 gram of fat. Voilà! You have a product that's 99 percent "fat free," with 100 percent of its calories from fat. This example is, of course, hypothetical. But "2% milk" is indeed 98 percent fat free, yet 45 of its 130 calories in a cup (almost a third) are fat. Check it out.

The most important information on the label is the number of calories per serving and the number of fat calories. This ratio gives you the *real* fat content. For example, turkey or ham that's labeled "96% fat free" contains only 50 calories per 1-ounce serving, but 15 of them are fat calories. This means that nearly a third of its total value is acquired from fat.

- *No cholesterol* means that a food contains 0 grams of cholesterol. Zip. Zero. But again, terms such as "no fat," "healthy," "diet," "new and lighter," and "low calorie" merely *imply* no or low cholesterol, which is exactly what the manufacturers want you to believe. Get in the habit of checking the numbers on the back to be sure that the cholesterol count really is nil.
- *No salt added* is another label meant to bamboozle the unaware. Condiments such as mustard and vinegar don't *need* any added salt, and dairy products such as milk and cheese are naturally high in sodium. If your physician has recommended that you avoid salt, don't settle for anything less than a "salt free" label, and check the fine print for the amount of sodium.

Diets Are Deceptive

It may be no coincidence that "scam" and "diet" are both four-letter words. With a third to a half (depending on which survey you believe) of Americans fighting the battle of the bulge, any product that promotes weight loss has a huge target audience. We're currently besieged by an entire diet industry: books, exercise equipment and programs, foods, and pills. Indeed, they may offer some genuine benefits, but if you're a buyer, beware! And when you seek a solution, think long term.

Although some publishers may claim that diet books are dead, you would never think so when strolling through one of the new super bookstores. Shelves abound with weight-loss information, all guaranteed to help the poor dieter lose pounds, supposedly for good. What's important to remember is this: Every diet works!

For a while. Whether it distinguishes itself with an emphasis on low calories, low fat, low cholesterol, or high fiber, nearly every published diet does indeed enable you to lose pounds, as long as you stay with the program. The problem is that if you want to maintain your new weight, you have to eat significantly fewer calories than you did before you began the diet. Quite simply, the body resists change. When we either add or subtract pounds in a short period of time, our bodies do their best to reverse the trend and get back to "normal." Researchers have found that if you want to maintain a 10 percent reduction in weight, you will have to consume not 10 percent, but *20 to 25 percent* fewer calories—for a lifetime!

Clearly that is no easy proposition. As soon as a weight goal is attained and that low-fat scoop of cottage cheese or tofu or yogurt is replaced by what most of us consider "normal" fare, back comes the lost weight with a vengeance! Staying slim is not impossible, but it requires constant vigilance, including a permanent commitment to exercise, particularly weight training. Aerobics do produce more immediate results, but pumping iron makes a critical difference in the long run because muscles burn more calories than fat. The higher your muscle-to-fat ratio, the more efficient your metabolism and the easier you can shed excess weight.

Most books now address the "yo-yo" syndrome, and many espouse a permanent "eating plan" as opposed to a diet. But the simple fact is that altering our eating habits for the long haul is easier said than done. Book jackets and ads are created for the sole purpose of making sales, and to that end they'll promise anything, even eternal slimness. So before you shell out your hard-earned cash for the latest flavor-of-the-month diet, be sure you're motivated to make a long-term commitment. Otherwise, the promise of a "new you" might well end up being—perish the thought—just a chubbier version!

THE "CONTAMINATED WATER" CAPER

The basic element of nutrition is water. It's more essential than food, and increasing attention is being paid to its quality. But even those who swear by Evian and Perrier occasionally use tap water for cooking, tea, or coffee, and countless others drink it daily. A "safe water" scam that has been successful in various parts of the country is especially slick because the swindlers come equipped with such impressive props. It works like this:

When a homeowner answers a knock on the door, he or she is greeted by a clean-cut, professional-looking young man or woman. "I hate to bother you," he says, "but our department's been getting calls about contaminated tap water. If I can just get a sample I can run a quick test right on the spot to see if your water supply is safe."

Nobody in his or her right mind wants to drink water with little bugs swimming around in it. Hence, the homeowner almost always responds according to script and leads the fellow into the kitchen. There the guy opens his kit, takes out a vial, and fills it with water from the tap. He adds a drop of this and a drop of that, and abracadabra, he's got a "reading." (What he's really added to the tap water is a dose of bacteria.)

Uh-oh. Things don't look so good. But the scam artist doesn't expect you to take him at his word. "Come take a look," he says, inviting the water drinker to inspect the contents of the tube with a microscope. Of course you look at the stuff you and your family (even the baby!) have been blithely swigging down. What you see is not a pretty sight. Things with legs on them are swimming around in *your* water (and no doubt in your stomach!). With these images racing through your head, you turn to the "official" the way a drowning man reaches for an extended hand. "What do we do?"

Your worst fears are eased by a reassuring smile. Not to worry, there's no cause for alarm—yet. The situation's going to be taken care of, and in the meantime, there's always the option of bottled or purified water. There's just a one-time charge for the water evaluation. A small price to pay for avoiding a plague of microscopic monsters. Still shaken, you do what most right-thinking bacteriaphobes would do—write a check.

Don't let your fear of unwelcome guests in your tap water allow you to invite another kind of creepy visitor into your home. Before allowing anyone to perform a test, check with the Department of Water and Power or the appropriate agency in your district.

Is Bottled Water Better?

When confronted with concerns about municipal drinking water, most people simply put their fears to rest by switching to a bottled product. But is the water in glass or plastic containers really safer and purer? Or is that just what advertisers would like us to think?

Bottled water can cost as much as 700 times more than water from the tap, creating plenty of motivation to "puff" the product. Marketing experts have done a good job of convincing us that anything in a bottle is automatically superior. In the 1980s bottled water sales increased 400 percent and are still on the rise. But what are we really buying for those extra dollars?

There are no laws requiring that bottled water meet standards higher than those for tap water. Some of it is plain old municipal water that has been filtered and packaged with a fancy (and comforting) label. Much like wines that are bottled at the chateau, a number of designer waters boast that they are "bottled at the source." The phrase immediately conjures images of bubbling springs and waterfalls, glistening in the sunlight with radiant purity. But as aesthetically appealing as that "source" may be, it is no guarantee of quality. In 1987 one well-known sparkling water was found to contain radioactivity that exceeded legal limits.

If you're concerned about a particular brand-name water, your options for obtaining information are limited. The FDA has no database or 800 numbers for consumers to call. What you can do is contact the manufacturer and request test results and other detailed data. Then read the information carefully and compare it to that of competitors. You might also check articles in *Consumer Reports*. Or just drink tap water and take your chances.

OVER-THE-COUNTER "REMEDIES"

If you think that snake-oil salesmen disappeared along with the horse and buggy, think again. They continue to practice their trade but have adapted to more sophisticated times. Despite today's state-of-the-art medicine, there's a thriving market for alternative treatments. Natural remedies, ranging from homeopathic cures to vitamins and herbs and glandular materials, are sold in health food stores, grocery marts, and mail order catalogs as well as mainstream discount and club stores.

Leaders in the field of alternative medicine, such as the controversial Nobel Prize winner Linus Pauling, espoused the benefits of supplements such as vitamin C years before "antioxidant" became a household word. And natural-health practitioners were among the first to decry the overuse of antibiotics, a practice that now even the most traditional factions admit has resulted in drug-resistant bacteria.

Today many of us are choosing to educate ourselves on health matters: We get second, third, and even fourth opinions; we read labels and brochures that accompany over-the-counter and prescription drugs; and, when appropriate, we augment traditional medicine with complementary or alternative care. The key word here is "educate." Those who read diligently and objectively and heed the observations of a variety of experts may well succeed in improving their health and quality of living.

In 1994 Congress passed a law limiting the claims that can be made on labels of supplements and nonprescription drugs. Tremendous resistance to this bill was voiced by consumers who were "certain" that its passage would cause all supplements to be removed from the shelves. That, of course, has not happened, but the makers of these products are now more restricted in their advertising claims.

Still, the hype goes on. Those who purchase a health product through the mail find themselves inundated with countless brochures and catalogs offering an array of products that promise, in vague, carefully worded statements, to restore everything from hair to virility.

Manufacturers get around the law by stating, "a recent study shows . . ." The catch is that studies and statistics can be easily manipulated to substantiate manufacturers' claims. What you should remember is that no single study proves anything except the need for further research. One isolated trial can include errors resulting from an unusually high placebo effect, erroneous premises, or even intentionally falsified data. If, however, repeated successful studies on animals are followed by comprehensive human trials that test for both for efficacy and side effects, then we may be on to something.

Above all, don't make decisions based on anecdotal material. An all-too-common fallacy is the belief that "correlation" means "causation." For example, 98 percent of all those who died in the past week probably consumed tap water. That doesn't mean our water supply is contaminated. And we often hear someone say, "He took this product and his symptoms cleared up overnight." There are many ailments that randomly come and go, and others that eventually resolve on their own with or without treatment. So even if a particular herb or vitamin regimen seems to have eased your last bout with the flu, at least entertain the possibility that you might simply have had a mild case. On the other hand, if acupressure or massage consistently reduces your headache pain, it would seem wise—or at least harmless—to continue.

Most of us want to be as responsible as possible for our own health, as well we should. Here are a few guidelines to steer you through the fierce competition of over-the-counter tonics and treatments.

- Don't purchase any product solely on the basis of one study.
- Beware of products that claim to cure everything from cancer to acne.
- Watch out for the claim "all natural," which doesn't guarantee anything. It can describe hemlock and heroin.
- Remember that celebrities aren't medical experts. And they are generally well paid for their promotional appearances in commercials and infomercials.
- Be aware that some normally benign over-the-counter medicines can become toxic when mixed with prescription drugs. Be sure your doctor and pharmacist are aware of *everything* you are taking, including vitamins, herbs, and nonprescription products.
- And most important: Don't abandon conventional medical therapies for unproven remedies if you are battling a serious illness.

A word about "organic" food. Everything we eat, except salt and water, is organic, which means "natural." Thus the phrase "organic food" (which is usually more costly than other produce) is meaningless. It implies that a crop is grown without artificial fertilizers or pesticides. But wait a minute. Does that mean farmers might use horse manure or cow dung? With bugs crawling on it? Yes, that's exactly what it means.

Remember, "organic" farming was the only way food was grown back in the good old days, when life expectancy was decades shorter than it is today.

2

LEGAL LAND MINES

In an age where political correctness is carried to extremes (at least one newspaper won't even use the term "Dutch treat") it's still open season when it comes to lawyer bashing. And in many instances there's good reason.

Obviously we all know fine attorneys who work hard and maintain their sense of ethics. But there is an undeniable basis for the dozens of variations on the old joke: When his boat capsized, why wasn't the lawyer eaten by the sharks? Professional courtesy!

Many people in the legal profession do take shameless advantage of their clients, possibly because they know they have a captive audience. It's easy enough to change barbers or dry cleaners, but if you're in the middle of litigation you're pretty much at your attorney's mercy. We all know that we should check out a prospective lawyer before handing over a retainer. Yet all too often, time and circumstances are pressing, and the sense of urgency prevents us from gathering references and recommendations. But careful selection of an attorney is the best way to avoid some of the outrageous but perfectly legal rip-offs listed below.

Double-Billing Hours

While most of us don't have to worry about hiring someone like Robert Shapiro or F. Lee Bailey any time soon, even an ordinary attorney charges several times the hourly rate of most certified public accounts, psychotherapists, and even plumbers!

But the damage doesn't stop there. What most people don't realize is that less-than-scrupulous lawyers sometimes send out billings for more than twenty-four hours a day. Sound far-fetched? Unfortunately, it's common enough to have inspired this old joke: A young attorney complained to St. Peter about arriving in heaven at the tender age of thirty-seven. St. Pete checked his records carefully and replied, "But according to your billing hours, you're seventy-five!"

In poorly paid (by comparison) areas of the law such as insurance defense and domestic relations, where there is a volume practice, it's commonplace for attorneys to make court appearances on four or five cases in one day and then bill each client for the entire eight hours. Here's one example of how it works:

Let's say you've been involved in a traffic incident and need to be represented in court. After a sleepless night you dress in your best suit and meet your counsel on the courthouse steps. Then you nervously enter the courtroom—and wait. And wait. Sometimes the delay requires you and your umpteen-dollar-an-hour attorney to sit for several hours until your case is called.

And each minute you wait, the clock ticks away and your fees pile up. But while you sit there squirming, perhaps wondering if it might not be cheaper to start a new life in some country that doesn't have an extradition treaty with the United States, your attorney is busy "making hay."

He or she may very well be passing the time working on a brief for another client! At the end of the week you'll receive a hefty invoice for those hours in court, and so will the client whose brief was being drafted. Double time, double money.

One way to avoid being victimized is to insist that your attorney give you an estimate of total hours and costs *before* you start. If the costs sound high, you might ask how much he or she charges for a particular procedure. Then call four or five other attorneys and inquire what they charge. If, for example, the average cost of a motion in court is $350, and your lawyer charges $500, tell him or her so at the outset. Make it clear that he or she doesn't have carte blanche when it comes to billing.

If you feel you've been taken advantage of by a legal eagle, it should be comforting to know that bar associations throughout the country have been cracking down on this kind of double-timing. If you have a complaint, contact an arbitration board within your state's bar association.

INCREMENTAL BILLING

Incremental billing is another way attorneys can leave their teethmarks on clients. This can "nickel and dime" invoices up to astronomical levels. For example, many firms bill in fifteen-minute increments. That means that if your lawyer so much as opens a piece of correspondence related to your case, glances at a fax, or takes a thirty-second phone call, you get billed for no less than a quarter hour. Some dare to bill when a call comes in and the attorney is out of the office. I even know of one authenticated case where an attorney programmed his phone automatically to dial clients every fifteen minutes, all day long, or until they answered. When they finally picked up, the lawyer then billed for each call. If the client was away for any length of time, those quarter-hour fractions added up to one scary statement! And if that's not enough, sometimes a photocopy can cost you as much as 50¢ or even $1 per page.

It's a good idea to know the ground rules when you begin a relationship with an attorney. Ask exactly how billing is done, what services you will be expected to pay for, and at what rate. If there's ever a time to negotiate, it's now, not later.

ADOPTION FRAUDS

Choosing to adopt a child is one of the most important and life-altering decisions a family can make. And because many couples select this option after years of painful disappointments, they are especially vulnerable to scams.

Of all the schemes in existence, those that deceive prospective parents may be the cruelest of all. One example of such emotional manipulation involved a pregnant young woman in the Chicago area who contacted at least five adoption agencies regarding placement of her unborn child. In good faith, she was put in touch with several couples. All of them desperately wanted a child and were willing to make generous provisions for the mother.

One trusting couple handed over more than $3,000 to cover her maternity expenses. And so did five other childless couples, each believing they would become the adoptive parents. All six couples rewarded the young woman's acting performance with cash, and those from out of state even sent her plane tickets and waited for her at the airport.

In all, the successful scam netted the mother-to-be more than $20,000 in cash and airline tickets over seven months. Worse yet was the emotional pain suffered by the couples who were joyously awaiting parenthood.

If you are considering adoption, be sure you work with agencies and/or attorneys who make certain that all the legal paperwork is in order. And don't hesitate to check and double-check on the legitimacy of anyone, individual or agency, who requests money. You can start by calling the National Adoption Center at (800) 862-3678. If they don't have information on a specific agency, they will refer you to an organization that does.

Long-Lost "Relatives"

It was the happiest day in Susie's life. Her most cherished dream had always been to locate her father, an American soldier who brought her mother to the United States and then disappeared after Susie was born. Like many children who were the result of wartime romances, Susie hoped to satisfy her longings and meet her father and his family. An only child, she especially fancied the idea that she might have half-sisters and -brothers, perhaps in a nearby city.

After appearing on a national talk show and declaring her desire to locate her father, Susie received the call she'd been waiting for. A friendly sounding woman claimed she'd seen Susie on television and was convinced that she was her long-lost stepsister. A meeting was arranged, and the "sister" quickly succeeded in winning Susie's confidence. She even persuaded her to make a down payment on a car, assuring Susie that their father would reimburse her. The next day the stranger made a hasty exit from Susie's life, with the new car.

Eventually convicted of fraud, this skillful imposter confessed to a number of adoption-related scams. And she apparently had no shortage of victims. There's a growing number of adults like Susie who, through adoption or abandonment, have been separated from one or more of their birth parents and are now trying to reconstruct family ties. Because these individuals are so emotionally vulnerable, they are easy targets for cruel hoaxes.

If you are seeking to locate either your birth parents or children you gave up for adoption, consult the National Adoption Registry at (800) 875-4347 or an attorney. And no matter who initiates contact, never hand over money or valuables to strangers until you've thoroughly investigated them.

Doctors Who "Doctor" Workers' Comp Claims

When we think of malpractice, we usually conjure visions of a sponge left in a surgical patient. But some shady physicians try to involve patients in workers' comp insurance or disability scams. While those of the older generation were taught to revere physicians, today more and more of us are learning to question them. Many patients now visit their doctors armed with a list of sophisticated questions, and it's considered routine to request a second opinion on serious matters.

But while many of us concern ourselves with getting the best possible health care, we rarely walk into a doctor's office expecting him or her to be involved in outright fraud. And while they count for only a small fraction of the medical community, there are a few physicians who unscrupulously take part in insurance scams.

With the challenge of trying to make a profit under managed care plans, there is an increasing temptation for today's doctors to cut corners. For example, suppose a factory worker shows up at his internist's office complaining of lower back pain. This ailment is one of the most common reasons for office visits and will affect a majority of the population in the course of a lifetime. While an honest doctor might assess such a patient and recommend that he lose his pot belly and do some back-strengthening exercises, the practitioner hoping to create a disability claim might question his patient about his job. Does he work in an awkward position? Has he ever fallen at work? Does he regularly put in overtime?

Although this kind of scam doesn't directly harm the patient, we all end up paying the price through increased insurance premiums. And of course such doctors benefit by billing insurance companies for treatments and diagnostic procedures that the patient doesn't really need and that may last for months.

Some back pain is caused or at least aggravated by work-related tasks, but in many cases weight loss and exercise are enough to bring about significant improvement. You should beware of the doctor whose line of questioning seems to lead into murky legal areas or who encourages you to admit to vague symptoms that may have nothing to do with your job. While the idea of drawing disability compensation might be tempting, unless complaints are valid, don't even think about conspiring with a less-than-scrupulous doctor. To do so could foster yet another ailment—one big headache resulting from complicity in the commission of fraud.

3

SENIOR CITIZEN SCAMS

Home Protection Hoaxes

The desire for independence coupled with the fear of helplessness makes senior citizens easy marks for telemarketers hawking home safety and self-protection products. A recent crackdown on an operation in California and Texas put the spotlight on a common type of boiler-room scam.

A senior citizen, perhaps living alone or with an elderly spouse, receives a phone call. She's told that she's won a valuable prize. But in order to collect the goods, she must purchase one or more home safety products. The merchandise might include emergency packs, earthquake kits (big in California), flame retardant sprays, fire extinguishers, or various alarm systems.

Of course there's nothing wrong, per se, in selling these products. But sometimes big telemarketing rings peddle their wares almost exclusively to those over sixty-five, charge many times what the item is worth, and, worst of all, employ strong-arm tactics.

Now let's assume that our lucky lady says thanks but no thanks to the prize she's allegedly won. With a polite good-bye she starts to hang up. If that's the end of it, there's no problem. But scamsters don't let their victims off the hook so easily.

Abusive lines often sound something like this:

"If you don't have some flame retardant spray handy you could burn alive. If you care so little about yourself, think about your husband!"

Or: "Without an emergency kit you could get an infection and end up with gangrene by the time you get to a doctor. I know a woman who lost her leg that way."

By playing on the elderly's greatest fears, these hucksters often succeed in browbeating older people into paying outrageous prices for products they become convinced they can't live without. And if a senior happens to be easily confused or submissive, it's all the more despicable.

An answering machine that screens calls may be the best protection against these household pests.

"Friends" You Meet on the Phone

With the increasing focus on street crime, many of us, young and old alike, live in fear of physical violence. We put bars on our windows and extra locks on the doors, and we keep our money stashed safely in the bank. But the sound of a gunshot, a strange car circling the neighborhood, or a knock on the door after dark can quickly cause us to panic. And this is especially true for the isolated older person who often feels, in today's brutal world, that his or her home is under siege.

The telephone, on the other hand, is a welcome friend, a source of communication with loved ones and a link to immediate help should there be a crisis. Rarely do we consider the telephone in the same light as an unlocked door. And yet it can be just that, a ready port of entry for smarmy schemers.

Older persons, particularly those who are lonely and living by themselves, are at special risk. Unlike the immediate sense of violation one feels when a home is physically broken into, many people are unaware of trespass by telephone while the act is in progress. It can happen like this:

An eightysomething woman lives alone and prizes her independence.

She knows how to take care of herself. When boiler-room salespeople call and try to interest her in Florida swampland, she quickly dispatches them with a polite but firm "no." She's not about to toss her grandchildren's inheritance away on some phony investment scheme.

But the evenings sometimes get lonely. Her children and grandchildren are attentive, but they are busy trying to juggle work, school, and family. So when the phone rings and a shy-sounding young salesman apologizes for bothering her, she hesitates before hanging up. He graciously accepts her "Sorry, I'm not interested" and explains that he's new in town and working hard at a job he's not thrilled about. He admits that selling isn't really his cup of tea, but he's a long way from home and trying to get situated in a big, unfriendly city. Poor kid.

The woman listens to his story and offers a bit of friendly advice. Maybe she recommends a singles' club her son once belonged to or a church where the young man can meet some nice people. He's appreciative and mentions that she reminds him of his grandmother, who, God rest her soul, died last year. Before hanging up, he asks if maybe he could call her again sometime, just to chat.

Why not?

He phones the woman a few days later and tells her how much she cheered him up the other night. It's comforting to have a friendly voice to talk to when you're all alone. The woman confesses that she sometimes feels the same way. It's not that she doesn't have family and friends, it's just that everyone is so busy and she hates to take up too much of their time. She's happy to be talking with someone who's a good listener, who doesn't seem driven by the clock.

She's surprised and delighted when flowers arrive from her young "phone mate." Nothing ostentatious, just a nice little arrangement to brighten up her living room. When he calls again, she thanks him, and he listens patiently while she tells him about her latest bout with arthritis. Not wanting to bore him, she turns the conversation to politics, or books, or music and finds they have common interests.

More and more, the lonely woman looks forward to her conversations with the young man and is pleased and flattered when he sends her another gift. And she rejoices with him when he announces that he hopes to land another job soon, one with some real potential.

A few days later he calls excitedly and tells her about his new position with a big marketing firm. He's been hired on a provisional basis, so he needs to make some quick sales to prove his worth.

It doesn't matter what he's selling or what the angle is. It might be an appliance or shares in a South African diamond mine. There are dozens of variations. The woman now considers the salesman a friend, so all her normal barriers are down. And be assured, after spending time and money cultivating their relationship, the nice young man will be after more than a little change.

As we go through life we all need to be open to new friendships, for each one brings a special meaning to our lives. But seniors especially should be wary of any relationship that begins with a sales pitch. The caller's original agenda isn't likely to change. Again, an answering machine that screens calls can be extremely helpful; most salespersons hang up when they hear a message, and friends and family can announce themselves.

Real Estate Offers from Strangers

Sometimes independence, a quality that senior citizens cherish highly, can be their undoing, especially when approached by a calculating scam artist. One unusually robust man lived by himself, managed his own affairs, and was physically active. By all measures he was mentally alert and still had a vital interest in world affairs. In nearly nine decades he had seen horse-and-buggy days evolve into the space age.

Having struggled through the Depression, he was thrifty to a fault, living modestly on Social Security and stock dividends. Years before, for just a few hundred dollars, he had purchased a small lot in Laguna Beach, a seaside community in California's affluent Orange County. Because the hillside property was oddly shaped and not well situated for building, he had let it remain undeveloped.

One day, out of the blue, he received a call from a real estate investor who claimed he was buying property in the area. This wily character began his bidding low; he offered the man twice what he had originally paid for his lot. Comfortable with his meager but secure existence, this senior citizen saw nothing wrong with doubling his money on what he considered a nearly worthless piece of real estate. In spite of his savvy in many areas, his comprehension of inflated property values, especially during California's real estate heyday, was a bit behind the times.

And that, of course, is what the buyer was banking on. He pressured for a quick consummation of the deal, before the man had time to consult with his family. By the time he got around to mentioning the deal to his son, it was a fait accompli.

Such Machiavellian investors make regular visits to the Hall of Records to determine ownership of valuable properties. With a little sleuthing (such as checking voter registration), it's easy enough to establish a person's age. And when these bottom dwellers discover that a choice lot has been owned for decades by someone well up in years, they call and make a dirt-cheap offer. If they're lucky, and they often are, they acquire the property for a fraction of its worth.

Never sell real estate to an unsolicited buyer without first getting an appraisal from a real estate professional and checking county property tax records for the latest assessed value. You should be vigilant and keep an eye on assets that might be targeted by slick operators.

Products that Promote "Male Vigor"

Although impotence occasionally strikes younger men, it's definitely a problem that increases with age. Therefore, older men are a prime target for "male rejuvenating formulas." In recent years the FDA put a stop to sales of a product with the dubious name of Crocodile Penis Pills. But there are countless other concoctions on the market that claim to restablish male vigor.

Most of these potions are harmless. In fact, some even boast (in small print) that they contain a "famous placebo," counting on the fine print remaining unread or on the senior not knowing that a placebo is a neutral substance that sometimes produces psychological effects. But there are other products that are not so benign. Some include procaine hydrochloride in their mix, which can cause allergic reactions, and an herb called yohimbine, known to induce a variety of serious ailments and thought to be especially risky for the elderly.

Doctors in Europe have been administering testosterone injections to energize older male patients, and some U.S. doctors are following their lead. And there are other drugs, including antidepressants and growth hormones, that show promise. But like estrogen for women, hormone replacement for men is not without risk. For example, it's believed that testosterone shots may encourage prostate cancer. Clearly, more study is needed.

So if life and love aren't what they used to be, see a good physician and discuss all the physical and psychological aspects of your condition. And stay away from over-the-counter goop that promises to put a tiger in your tank.

Ëmergency Alarm Systems

Recently, Ellie thought her worst nightmare had come true. The nearly eighty-year-old grandmother slipped as she was stepping out of the shower and lay on the floor in pain, unable to get to her feet. The sensation of helplessness was aggravated when her phone rang, just a few feet out of reach.

Fortunately for Ellie, a neighbor stopped by within the hour and heard her cries for help. Luckily, her fall resulted in nothing worse than bruises and a sprained back. But she and her family were well aware of how much worse it might have been.

That evening Ellie saw a TV commercial pitching an emergency device she could use to alert family or neighbors in just such a situation. She called the 800 number almost immediately and requested more information about the product. But not much was forthcoming. When she asked that she be sent a brochure, she was told that the device was sold only through in-home presentations.

Well, then, what about the price?

The saleswoman on the line wasn't about to part with that information either. She said that a safety "counselor" would discuss payments during the appointment. Nobody's fool, Ellie normally wouldn't have agreed to the demonstration without receiving more input, but she was still badly shaken from her near tragedy. A few choice phrases from the representative reinforced her apprehensions, and a time was set.

The next afternoon a young man arrived with the alarm system and proceeded to show Ellie why she couldn't afford to live another day without the device. The unit had a receiver that connected to the telephone, and a portable "panic button." In an emergency, Ellie could press the button and her phone would automatically dial for help.

On the surface this sounds like a much-needed and possibly life-saving product sold to the perfect customer. The question for Ellie (and she had to ask more than once) was the cost. As much as she wanted to buy the unit, Ellie's budget was limited, and she thought she should consult with more than one company before making a purchase. A wise decision, but not one the salesman was about to let her make.

Like the guest who came to dinner, the young man stayed and stayed. And as Ellie repeatedly requested time to "think it over," his pitch became more aggressive. "You could fall again tonight," he grimly warned, "and lie there for days." Finally, as he was trained to do, the salesman wore her down. Ellie signed on the infamous dotted line and agreed to pay an inflated price for something she could have obtained, through other sources, for far less.

Most monitoring systems are sold or leased through hospitals and health care agencies rather than directly to customers. If you are considering an emergency alert device, first contact your physician, local hospital, or the Visiting Nurse Association. In addition to supplying units, they may be able to recommend inexpensive yet effective devices new to the market. In cases of postoperative patients, where disability is temporary, renting or leasing a unit might be the best solution. For long-term use, some systems can be leased for as long as three years. Acquisition through these sources is almost certain to be less expensive than buying from a private company. Some of these opportunistic vendors have been known to size up potential customers' homes and valuables before quoting a price, and then go for broke.

If you do decide to buy an emergency system from a private company, do the following:

- Demand a price list and a printed description of the equipment and the service it provides. (And don't take no for an answer.)
- Check out the firm through the Better Business Bureau, to determine if there have been any complaints.

- Discuss your decision with family, friends, and your local emergency or 911 system. Make certain they are willing and able to respond appropriately in an emergency should you choose not to have the company itself monitor the system. Know that in most states you have three days to cancel any contract entered into with a door-to-door salesperson.

THE LAST LAUGH

While senior citizens are usually the target of scams, once in a while a notable elder will inadvertently get the better of someone. I'm reminded of Madame Calment, a ninety-year-old Frenchwoman who, having outlived her heirs, was approached by a fellow with an unusual business proposition.

This man offered to pay Madame's mortgage every month until she died—a legitimate arrangement in exchange for receiving ownership of her property after her demise. The agreement surely must have seemed like a shrewd deal to the fellow, who no doubt counted on acquiring the real estate for only a few thousand dollars. After all, the lady was ninety. How much longer could she live?

Some thirty years later, after paying out twice what the apartment was worth, this man receives an annual note from Madame Calment, containing a charming apology for her celebrated longevity. In February 1995, in a nursing home in Arles, France, the lady, wit and wisdom still intact, celebrated her latest birthday, number 120!

Along with cake and champagne, I hope Madame is enjoying a well-deserved last laugh!

4
Travel
Trickery

Falling victim to a scam is a surefire way to ruin a vacation. Knowing what to do, and what to avoid, can save your time, money, and sanity. If you're contemplating a tour or travel package of any kind, it's important to read brochures with a wary eye. Tours that promise that you'll "see" the Louvre may very well mean that you'll only catch a glimpse of the famous museum as the bus rolls by and your tour guide shouts, "There's the Louvre!"

Any knowledgeable travel agent can fill you in on what the jargon really means so you'll have a clear idea of what to expect and know that "see" doesn't mean the same as "visit." You also need to take a careful look at the number of days offered on a trip. One tour may advertise twelve days, another only ten. But the longer trip may include travel days. For example, tours that are put together in England may list only the actual number of sightseeing days, but those originating in other counties are likely to include flight and travel days.

It also is important to determine the location of the hotels where you'll be staying. Some tours are priced lower because they offer less expensive lodging. But if you're stashed away in the boonies, what you save in hotel bills you may end up spending on taxi fares. You should also inquire about meals. Some eating plans allow you to select any item you wish from the menu, while others restrict you to communal fare. If you're in Paris and your mouth is watering for boeuf Bourguignon and all you're allowed is croque monsieur (a grilled ham-and-cheese sandwich), you're going to be disappointed.

TELEMARKETERS BEARING GIFTS

Under the provisions of a new law, the Federal Trade Commission now requires telemarketers selling vacations over the phone to make full disclosure of all the details and contingencies, including all costs, all conditions, and the circumstances under which you may cancel and/or receive a refund. But as we well know, scams continue to flourish in spite of the law, so we must constantly be on the alert.

Any voice over the phone that promises too-good-to-be-true travel rates should be thoroughly checked out. If you're offered a bargain rate cruise or free round-trip plane fares, never accept them at face value. Firms often offer travel incentive certificates for round-trip tickets. The only requirement is that the traveler purchase lodging from the company and pay in advance. In a number of instances, customers never receive their tickets and have to wage a battle to win reimbursement from their credit card company.

The following tips will help prevent your name from joining the list of travel-scam victims:

- If you're offered a deal that requires you to prepay processing fees, just say no.
- Never submit to pressure to close a deal on the spot. If you hear the words "this offer ends tonight at midnight," take your money and run.
- Not all telemarketers are dishonest. But if you decide to do business over the phone, do some serious checking. Call the hotels, air-

lines, or cruise ships involved and make sure they have received your deposit, then reconfirm every detail.

• Don't give financial information or credit card or bank account numbers to strangers over the phone or by fax or mail.

• The safest way to ensure a headache-free journey is to deal with reputable and well-known travel agencies.

"BARGAIN" MERCHANDISE

If you're traveling to Southeast Asia you can expect to be touched by the graciousness of the people. But be wary of those would help separate you from your money.

A couple from Denver were charmed when their Bangkok taxi driver (so different from those in New York) chatted about his family and offered pictures of his beloved children. Then he mentioned his uncle who happened to own a little shop just around the corner. Uncle Joe, as he fondly called him, would sell them jewelry and designer watches at bargain prices.

Thinking they had an "inside opportunity" here, the couple agreed to be driven to the small storefront. There they were shown a lady's dinner ring set with precious stones. Not totally naive, the Americans said, "Sorry, it's way over our budget."

The shop owner then countered with a lower price, and his customers responded in kind, the way they had learned in Mexico. They feigned a lack of interest and almost walked out. Just in the nick of time, the merchant reconsidered and offered the sparkling band to them at a rock-bottom price. Chalk one up for the tourists.

Well, not really.

What actually happened was that the couple fell for a common scam. Because the ring was so overpriced to begin with, what the Americans thought was skillful negotiating on their part was carefully calculated into the final (and still outrageous) price.

Although jewelry offered in the boutiques of the larger hotels is usually of high quality, it may not always be fairly priced. Watch out for large and small vendors alike. Even though labor costs are lower in Southeast Asia, be suspicious of a "rock-bottom" price tag on any designer merchandise or jewelry. And elaborate bargaining sessions where your skills are praised should send you running.

If you feel that you've been bamboozled by overpricing or fraudulent designer goods, here are a couple of things you might do:

- Contact the country's tourism authority and state your complaint.
- If you paid by credit card, contact the company and see if they will hold off paying the vendor until the matter has been investigated. But don't expect too much; in most cases you will have to chalk up your experience to the old axiom that "travel is broadening."
- Contact the United States Embassy and see what suggestions they offer. Your options will vary according to country.

Airport or Train Station Locker Key Scams

Recently a great-grandmother from Nebraska made her first train trip to Los Angeles to see her favorite niece's latest offspring. Recently widowed, she wasn't used to traveling alone, but she prided herself on her adventurous spirit.

The Amtrak train rolled ahead of schedule into downtown Los Angeles against a backdrop of smog and traffic. The woman accepted the conductor's help getting off the train and asked where she might store her suitcase while she got a bite to eat and waited for her ride.

He pointed her in the direction of the pay lockers, and off she went. Unfortunately, the only available lockers were in the top row. Although her spirit was willing, she didn't see how she could hoist up her heavy luggage. Fortunately, a nice-looking young man observed her struggle and offered to give her a hand.

She gratefully let him lift her valise into the locker. She opened her purse to offer him a dollar or two for his trouble, but he responded with a shake of his head and a big smile. "Don't even think about it!" he said graciously. Then, handing her the locker key, he wished her the traditional Los Angeles nice day.

When the woman's niece met her in the coffee shop a little later, they walked back to the lockers to pick up Granny's bag. The younger woman tried the key, but it didn't fit. Then she tried again. "Are you sure this is the right key?"

Finally they summoned an official who listened to the woman's story and shook his head. "We'll get the locker open for you, ma'am," he offered, "but I think you're going to be disappointed."

Sure enough, the locker was empty. The nice guy had pocketed her key and given her a bogus one.

But the plucky woman accepted her loss philosophically. "I should have been more careful," she confessed, "but he seemed like such a nice young man." Then, winking at her niece, she added, "I wonder how he'll look in my pink lace girdle!"

*B*RIBES IN *F*OREIGN *C*OUNTRIES

Many world-weary travelers have found that in Third World countries, bribery is a built-in part of the economy. Police officers and other officials often receive less than subsistence wages and depend on bribes the way American waiters rely on tips. In Mexico, for example, police officers are expected to pay for gas and upkeep on their patrol cars, and that takes a hefty chunk out of their already meager salary. In some countries, cops are expected to hand over a portion of their "take" to higher-ups, who in turn must kick back to their superiors.

Although palm greasing is less flagrant now than in the past, it still exists in various parts of the world. In some places drivers who look like tourists are frequently pulled over and charged with minor traffic offenses. Because we're all familiar with stories about the horrors of foreign jails, $20 or so seems like a small price to pay for freedom. And a crisp bill, readily offered, usually convinces an officer to be on his way. Occasionally, however, tourists find themselves facing the wrong end of a gun and "asked" to give more. In some instances, tourists are stopped by actual police, and in others, road bandits pose as law enforcement officials.

The worst situation, however, typically involves visitors who look young and hip. In certain countries youthful travelers are at special risk for being summarily restrained and accused of carrying drugs. Anyone who's seen the movie *Midnight Express*, about a young American's ordeal in a Turkish prison, will be chilled to the bone at the mere thought of a drug-related arrest in *any* foreign country.

If you find yourself in a ticklish situation, you can file a complaint with the United States Embassy or Ministry of Tourism—after the fact. But the best advice is to call the country's tourism bureau and our own State Department *before* traveling, so you can be as informed as possible about the traffic regulations, laws, and customs of each country you plan to visit.

Antiradiation Kits

Besides worrying about the plane actually crashing, white-knuckle flyers now have a new reason for queasiness—radiation poisoning. Or so some scammers would like you to believe.

One nervous flyer was browsing through an airport gift shop when she spotted an anti*radiation* kit. Anti*what*? She leafed through the literature and saw excerpts from a government report warning that frequent fliers accumulate more than miles; they may also increase their risk of cancer.

On the chance that her flight wouldn't go down in flames, this apprehensive passenger traded the last of her cash for assurance that air travel wouldn't do her in the slow way. When her seat belt was fastened and the flight attendant was describing the pleasures of a water landing, she opened her magic kit. Instead of a Buck Rogers–type head shield, our prudent passenger found a bottle containing "powerful agents" that would protect her from silent death. Vitamins. Heavy on antioxidants like C, A, and E, and time-released.

A reasonable dose of multivitamins probably won't do any harm, and many people place them in the chicken soup category—they can't hurt. But any generic brand would have cost far less than those few capsules packaged in the "antiradiation kit." And as for their efficacy or necessity, well, let's examine the facts.

What the crafty manufacturers did here was take a kernel of truth and embellish it with a healthy dose of puffery. Some studies have shown that flight crews may slightly increase their risk of cancer over the course of their careers. Radiation at cruising altitude is around a hundred times higher than on terra firma. Crew members who routinely circle the globe may incur a yearly dose of up to 900 millirems of radiation. While there's no hard evidence that this relatively low dosage is directly linked to cancer, projected statistics estimate one cancer death per one hundred crew members with a twenty-year exposure to 900 millirems annually.

As for infrequent flyers, the risk is even more minimal. On, say, a four-hour air excursion, you might absorb about 2 millirems, which results in a projected lifetime cancer risk of roughly one in a million.

We accept that there is a small risk in everything we do, including breathing anything but pure mountain air. And certainly the risk of driving to and from the airport far outweighs any threat posed by minuscule doses of radiation. So if you want to increase your chances of living into your nineties, spend your money on air bags for your car and always wear your seat belt. Oh, yes, try not to worry. You know what they say about stress.

Pest Repellents

"Boy, this elephant repellent really works!"

"How do you know?"

"Well, you don't see any elephants around, do you?"

It's good to keep this old joke in mind when you open your suitcase in an exotic locale. From pesky insects like no-see-ums in the Caribbean to snakes in India to spiders the size of dinner plates in South America, local critters can put a damper on vacation plans. And while bug repellent and mosquito netting may be appropriate in some parts of the world, it's not wise to shell out money for potions whose purpose and ingredients are in question.

Any good tourist guidebook should list hazardous creatures indigenous to a particular area. They usually offer sensible precautions (such as not wading in crocodile-infested swamps), along with remedies and preventive measures. Or you can ask your hotel concierge, travel agent, or tourist bureau for the information. Although you're unlikely to encounter snakes or other critters in modern hotels, such knowledge is a must if you plan to explore exotic terrains.

After-Hours Rip-Offs

Those who want to kick up their heels after hours may find that the pleasures of the night don't always come cheap. Social customs vary around the world, and in many nightclubs you may have to pay a lot more for an evening's entertainment than the traditional two-drink minimum.

And if you venture into the netherworld of red-light districts, you make yourself extra vulnerable to scams and rip-offs. After all, where would you take your complaints? In Bangkok, often called a "man's city" because of its easy access to ladies of the evening and exotic sex shows, many nightclubs impose an entertainment tax. A pair of tourists may find that the tab for few drinks runs well over $100. And if you try to "discuss" the matter with your waiter or the club manager, you may be greeted (or stopped from leaving) by some heavy muscle.

In Amsterdam's well-known legal red-light sector, women openly advertise their wares in showcased windows. It's not uncommon in some cities for a shill to take a man's money and send him to a designated room that turns out to be empty or nonexistent. One weary businessman searching for an after-hours drink in Montreal refused to hand over his money until he saw the central lights of the bell of the "Blind Pig" bar. He paid the cab driver and approached the lighted bell. When he reached it, that's all there was—a lighted bell attached to a battery and nothing else. And of course there are customers who have one too many drinks and wake up without their wallets and passports.

In Thailand, young girls are often sold into prostitution by families desperate for money, and now many of these teenagers have been diagnosed with AIDS. When you take into account the victimization that occurs in these situations as well as the formidable health and safety risks, the best advice is to stay out of harm's way.

The Taxi Scam

A small-town couple arrive in the Big Apple, suitcases in hand and a "golly-gee-whiz" grin on their faces. As they gaze around Penn Station wondering how they're going to secure a taxi, a smiling young man approaches.

"Need a taxi?"

Do they ever. "Can you take us to the Marriott near the theater district?"

No problem. "Twenty-five bucks. Trust me, you're not going to find anything cheaper."

The travelers nod, and the young fellow holds out his hand for the cash. Then he picks up their luggage and flags down a cab. He politely informs the driver of the pair's destination, helps hoist their bags into the trunk, then fades into the night.

Mr. and Mrs. Small Town chat amicably with the cab driver until they arrive at their midtown hotel. When he reads off the price on the meter (which is a fraction of $25), they explain that they've already paid his "friend."

Oh, how quickly the big city instructs us in the lessons of life!

Is Voicemail Really Private?

An executive who travels regularly spent a week in one of her favorite business-class hotels. During her visit she successfully wooed and won a new account and had a quick drink with an old boyfriend. When she returned home, ready to celebrate, her current flame greeted her with daggers.

"I thought it was over with Harry."

"What are you talking about?"

"He came by your hotel in Cleveland."

"Only for a drink. Wait a minute! How do you know that?"

It took the woman a while to convince her beau that her encounter was purely platonic. And it took him even longer to persuade her that he didn't have a private eye on her trail.

So, Sherlock, how did the fellow know—with four states between them—with whom the woman sipped a scotch and soda?

It seems that the boyfriend occasionally made business trips on which he stayed in the same hotel chain. Through frequent use he had become familiar with hotel's Voicemail system, which could be accessed by signaling the room number and first four letters of the lodger's last name. All he had to do was punch in the code, and he heard Harry's message asking the woman to join him in the bar.

Not only can the seriously suspicious use this method to check up on lovers and spouses, but business rivals can also listen in on "confidential" messages. Even bored hotel employees may occasionally amuse themselves by running in on intimate communications.

So how can you ensure the privacy of your messages when traveling? When you arrive at the front desk, request—and if necessary, *insist*—that your Voicemail code be changed, preferably to a personal code of your own choosing. It may cost you a generous tip, but peace of mind rarely comes at such a reasonable price.

METAL-DETECTOR THIEVES

A couple taking a cross-country flight with their two young children checked their luggage at the curb. Then they proceeded into the airport terminal and made their way toward the gate. As they approached the metal detector, the woman placed her handbag on the conveyer belt, and her husband did the same with his camera.

The kids and Mom passed through the detector with no trouble, then turned and watched as Dad set off buzzers. He removed the keys or coins from his pocket, then walked through again. Buzzers still rang. Embarrassed, and attracting more than a few stares, he tried to think what the offending item might be. Finally it was determined that the metal buttons on his jacket were the culprits. He was just happy they weren't on his underwear.

Laughing, the man and his wife each took a child by the hand and walked over to the conveyer belt to reclaim their possessions. The mom's handbag was there, but the camera was nowhere in sight. They walked around the belt, then asked the attendants for help. A quick search confirmed their worst fears: While attention had been focused on the commotion caused by the metal detector, someone had walked off with their expensive camera.

Because metal detectors are located in seemingly protected areas, travelers are often lulled into a false sense of security. Just as we clutch our wallets a little closer when walking down a dark street, the proximity of airport personnel tends to make us feel relaxed and off-guard. It is precisely this state of mind that encourages thieves and con artists to hover just ahead of passengers who are momentarily separated from their belongings.

Whenever you are parted, even briefly, from your possessions, always scan the area for those who might be lurking around, just waiting for an opportune moment. And most important, don't take your eyes off your valuables!

"Big Names" Can Be Deceptive

A New Hampshire woman started to throw out a certificate for a free Caribbean cruise that arrived in a pile of junk mail. Her first instinct warned her it was some kind of gimmick and should be tossed in the circular file. But her husband happened to see the expensively printed document and noticed that it bore the logo of one of the country's leading hotel chains.

"They're a public corporation," the man told his wife. "I don't think they'd be involved in anything that wasn't on the up-and-up."

His wife looked at the certificate again, and sure enough, there at the top was the gold embossed logo of a first-rate company. "Maybe we've got something here after all," she conceded.

The next day the woman called the number of the travel promoter and was told that the dates she desired for the cruise had been sold out. "June's a pretty busy month," the voice on the phone explained, "but what we can do is upgrade you to a deluxe cabin right on the top deck." The cost of the upgrade, of course, was more than enough to pay for the entire cost of the cruise.

At that point, the wife's original instincts kicked in, and she said thanks but no thanks. But she remained curious about hotel chain's participation in this questionable operation. After doing some research she found that many large corporations fail to screen all those who use their trademarks, especially if a firm is connected to an authorized franchise. Often they respond only when officially notified that a scam is being carried on in connection with their name.

Meanwhile, consumers continue to fall for schemes involving expensive upgrades, pitches for time-shares, or nonrefundable registration fees for trips that never materialize. If you receive an impressive-looking certificate stating that you've "won" or "will receive" a cruise, plane ticket, or free vacation, either call the parent company directly or take a tip from the New Hampshire lady—toss it.

5
Don't
Be a
Chump
for Charity

Giving to our fellow man should bring out the best in all of us. Unfortunately, man's humanity to man can prove to be fertile territory for creative scam artists. Before making out a check to an unfamiliar charity or other nonprofit organization, call the National Charity Information Bureau at (212) 929-6300 or the Council of Better Business Bureaus, Philanthropic Advisory Service at (703) 276-0100, and find out what portion of the receipts goes to administration and how much actually benefits the intended recipients.

Gifts with "No Obligation"

Some charities send out letters urging you to donate to their organization. Others send missives that include a bribe. One sensible but soft-hearted man received a roll of labels, complete with his name, address, and zip code. An accompanying promotional piece suggested that with the holidays approaching he might find them useful. There was no obligation, of course, but if he was so inclined, the nonprofit organization would appreciate any small cash gift he would care to bestow.

Although this man had no use for the labels, he didn't want to go to the trouble of sending them back by return mail. And therefore he felt that the honorable thing would be to pay for them with a small check. Once he responded, of course, he was promoted to the top of the foundation's donor list. From that moment on he was marked for a steady stream of unwanted and useless knickknacks, along with more emotional pleas to donate to the less fortunate.

In this case, the man was more honorable than he needed to be. The "gift exchange" is a ploy, where recipients of assorted tacky "gifts" are told there is "Absolutely no obligation. The gift is yours to keep, free of charge." Of course, the subtext comes through loud and clear: Only a cheapskate takes something for nothing.

In the broadest sense, this scheme falls under the umbrella of emotional blackmail. Not a nice tactic, but one that often works. So the next time you receive some kitschy trinket in the mail attached to a poignant request for a gift in return, just say no. You have no obligation whatsoever to pay, in any way, for a gift you did not request. If, on reading the enclosed literature, you decide that you would like to make a contribution, again you should call the National Charity Information Bureau at (212) 929-6300. This group will send you a phone number and information on the charity in question, so you can make an informed decision. If there is no substantive information available, it means the charity is probably fly-by-night and not worthy of your donation. Or a moment's worth of guilt.

Hypes from the Not Really Homeless

With the huge rise in the numbers of homeless Americans, organizations aren't the only ones seeking our charitable dollars. In any city of size, most of us have been approached by people on the street asking for help. While some of these people are worthy of our compassion and assistance, many behave in ways that cause us to view the homeless with anger and suspicion. Every situation is different.

Recently, a young couple was arrested after a long-running and highly profitable engagement on the streets. The man and woman were actually unemployed actors who decided to practice their craft by exploiting the kindness of strangers.

This team would approach passersby and offer, in their most winning manner, a hard-luck story that ended with a surefire grabber. The young woman, the couple confided, had just learned that she was two months pregnant. They would, of course, be eternally grateful for whatever help their "target" felt like giving.

For several months they "brought down the house," raking in a more-than-comfortable living with their finely honed skills. This pair might still be plying their trade if they hadn't encountered one of their donors for a second time. Not recognizing him, they repeated their tale of woe, complete with the punch line about the young woman being, amazingly, still just two months pregnant!

Authorities were notified, and the couple was forced to take their act off the road to a more confined area, behind bars. While sophisticated acts such as this may be rare, the streets are filled with hustlers, some of them with pretty clever pitches. When it comes to helping your fellow man or woman, it always comes down to a personal decision on a case-by-case basis. However, the best advice is to donate your charity dollars to reputable organizations with a well-known history of helping those truly in need.

Phony Delivery People

Charity usually implies helping those less fortunate than ourselves. But, as they say, charity begins at home, and to many good-hearted people, that means being a considerate neighbor. Unfortunately, one of the most common ways that neighbors help each other leaves them sitting ducks for a common scam.

A suburban woman was recently roused from her morning newspaper by an insistent doorbell. Clutching her robe around her, she opened the door to a pleasant man who explained that he had a package for her neighbor, who was not at home. Because the man next door happened to be a pilot and was frequently away, our good Samaritan was in the habit of taking in his packages and mail. When she was asked for a $20 COD charge, she quickly got her purse and took care of it.

When the pilot returned, he thanked his neighbor, repaid her the $20, and took his package inside. A few minutes later, he returned. "Do you have any idea who delivered this?" he asked. It seemed that his package contained nothing but a lot of newspapers and a couple of rocks.

The good neighbor was, of course, chagrined. But she was just one of many kind-hearted souls who, in their desire to help out, get helped out of a nice piece of change. In this particular instance, the "delivery man" was wearing a hat and a name tag and came equipped with an official-looking invoice for her to sign. Other such scamsters are daring enough to say they're with UPS or Federal Express and arm themselves with enough accoutrements to fool almost anyone.

How can you avoid this effective ploy? A good way to start is to hesitate before reaching for your wallet.

- If asked for money by a delivery person, insist on seeing the driver's vehicle. If a phone number is written on the side panel, excuse yourself and call the company. It should take only a minute or two to verify whether the delivery is for real.
- If you live in an apartment or condominium where no truck can be readily seen, ask for company ID and request the phone number. Most people hesitate to appear so distrusting, but this is not a popularity contest.
- If a delivery person can't satisfy your requests, tell him you're out of funds and he'll have to come back later.

THE "LADY IN DISTRESS" SCAM

Phony delivery people aren't the only slick operators who take advantage of good intentions. Unfortunately, the streets are full of those in search of easy targets.

When a councilman from a small town in the Midwest made his first trip to the Big Apple, he wasn't exactly a hayseed. He'd been warned about taxi drivers from hell, street hustlers, and other assorted rascals. So when he left a meeting and headed back to his hotel late one afternoon, he walked the New York walk and kept a sharp lookout for trouble.

But he was still a gentleman. When two elderly women walked toward him, he couldn't help noticing that one of them seemed to be struggling. The next moment the fragile lady collapsed on the sidewalk. Her friend bent over her, trying to elicit a response. As people gathered around, the out-of-towner stopped to offer assistance.

"I think she'll be all right," said the friend. "She gets these dizzy spells. . . ."

"Can I call an ambulance?"

"No, no, my sister and I live just around the corner. I think we can manage." And with that affirmation, the lady, with the gentleman's help, got her friend back on her tiny feet, and together, arms around each other, the ancient sisters trundled off. But not before they thanked the man for his kind help.

As the fellow entered the lobby of his hotel, he recalled a warning about pickpockets, checked for his wallet, and was relieved to find it safely in place. The big city wasn't as bad as people claimed. That night at dinner he dined with old friends and told the story of his sidewalk rescue. At which point one of his pals remarked, "Yeah, you still have your wallet, but did you count your cash?"

Startled, the visitor reached in his pocket and extracted his billfold. And as he examined his cash, his countenance changed from contentment to chagrin. He flipped through his wallet again, then dipped his hands into each of his pockets.

"Those sweet-faced little ladies!" he muttered through clenched teeth.

While the good Samaritan was assisting those two damsels in distress, their dexterous partner in crime had lifted his wallet, relieved him of his large bills, and carefully replaced the billfold. All in the twinkling of an eye.

I'm not suggesting that you cast a jaundiced eye at strangers in need of help. Disregard for human suffering is never in the best interests of individuals or society. But whenever you're mingling with crowds, whether it's on busy streets or at an event, make sure your cash and credit cards are secured in a waistband moneybelt or some other protected pocket.

Or if you really want to scam the scammers, you might keep an old wallet with a couple of Xeroxed hundred-dollar bills in a tempting spot. Just like the mugger who stole a man's package and found that it contained the contents of pooper-scooper duty, it's always nice when people get what they deserve!

CHARITY IMPOSTORS

Recently, a well-dressed woman in a red coat was approached by an earnest-looking solicitor outside a shopping mall. The pitch was classy and soft sell. "Please," said the young woman, "we'd really appreciate it if you could make just a small contribution to our shelter for abused women. We've been providing services for over five years and we're in danger of having to close down." Then she flashed an official-looking card and stated that all donations were tax deductible.

As the woman in red stood there for a moment apparently deliberating what to do, a couple walked by, listened to the appeal, and offered $20. As they walked away, she heard the woman say, "I don't usually give money out like that, but I know that organization, and it's really doing a lot of good. I'd hate to see them shut down."

The woman in the red coat felt the same way. That particular shelter was one of the best in the city, with less than 10 percent of collected funds going to administrative costs. It had a reputation for being well run and was considered a godsend to women who had no other options. For such a haven to be closed down would be a travesty.

But that wasn't likely to happen. The woman in scarlet just happened to be in charge of fund-raising for the shelter, and thanks to the efforts of many, it was operating in the black, without street solicitations. She studied the young woman for a minute, then said, "My checkbook is in the car." When she returned ten minutes later, police officer in tow, the scammer was gone.

Just be aware that those who want on-the-spot handouts are likely to be lining their own pockets. Even if they flash a certificate with an ID number, it could well be a fake. If there's a charity you favor, send a contribution. This is a case where "your check is in the mail" is good news for everybody.

The "Starving Children" Scam

When a crisis such as the one in Somalia makes headlines, scam artists and assorted sleazy characters crawl out en masse from under their respective rocks. Poignant photographs of starving children in newspapers and on the evening news instill most of us with guilt and compassion. We pause briefly in our busy schedules to reflect on the woes of the world and think, I wish there were something I could do.

So when a phone call comes in from a newly formed relief agency asking for a small donation, the response is often positive. Sometimes cash is requested, and in the name of expediency, a messenger is sent over to collect the money.

In some instances these outfits are outright fraudulent. The solicitors simply take the greenbacks and run. But many others operate just within the limits of the law, by obtaining a proper license and reporting their income. But when it comes to helping needy children, they hand over the bare minimum, perhaps 10 percent of their take, to a legitimate charity and use the other 90 percent to feed themselves. Unfortunately, a law that used to oblige charities to reveal the destination of collected monies was reversed by the United States Supreme Court in 1988.

Even when legitimate complaints are filed, little action may be taken. In many cities and counties, social service departments have limited budgets and staffs and are hard-pressed to investigate all those under suspicion.

The moral here is to donate your money to organizations with a proven track record. If there's a crisis anywhere in the world, you can rest assured that major charities such as the Red Cross and CARE will be working overtime. And they will gladly accept your check.

"Protection" from Phony Police

An immigrant family from Saigon was successful in starting a new life in Southern California. They used their savings to purchase a well-situated liquor store and soon had a thriving business. The father told his children, "What they say about America is true. This is a land of freedom and opportunity."

When a pair of fund-raisers walked into the store one day and requested a donation for the Deputy Sheriff's Association, the Vietnamese
gentleman felt he should contribute generously. He was grateful for the
chance to pursue his dreams in his new country and truly wanted to support his local government and police.

But his generosity doubled when the solicitors strongly hinted that
those who did not pitch in might expect "trouble." Familiar with police
tactics in some Asian nations, this store owner did not want to jeopardize
his new position, so he made sure his check was a large one.

Most police and sheriff departments do not solicit funds, and in this
instance they had no connection whatsoever to the heavy-handed fund-
raisers. And happily, the man from Saigon learned this fact in time,
when, in hopes of making a good impression, he decided to deliver his
donation personally to the sheriff's station.

Many targets of such scams are not so lucky. A lot of sleazy fund-
raisers single out immigrant neighborhoods, knowing that many foreigners carry with them well-founded fears of police misconduct.
Newcomers to this country should be especially wary of such tactics and
always verify organizations that are seeking money.

6

*A*UTOMOBILE *S*CAMS

Cars are such an essential part of modern life that their purchase, maintenance, and daily use affect nearly every aspect our lives. Whether it's crooked repair shops, tricky salesmen, or con artists on the road, vehicle-related scams seem to pop up everywhere. Here are a few you should be aware of.

*R*EAR-*É*ND *C*OLLISION *S*CAMS

If freeway snipers, drunk drivers, and people cruising along at 80 mph while shaving aren't enough to worry about, today's driver needs to be on the alert for accident scam artists. These rascals of the road who stage fraudulent accidents are highly organized and often work in pairs. When they spot a late-model car with a responsible-looking person at the wheel, they zero in like hunters during duck season.

While car number one, usually an old uninsured vehicle, positions itself just in front of you (the "mark"), car number two begins to cruise alongside. If all signs are go, the driver of car two honks at the target vehicle and gets your attention. You look over, and the scam artist smiles and points at your car, implying that you have a problem.

Concerned that you might have a bad tire or smoke pouring from your exhaust, you naturally try to figure out what's wrong. And while you're so occupied, car number one, the old jalopy in front of you, suddenly slams on his brakes. And you react, probably just a second too late.

As the perpetrator of a rear-end collision, you must now pull over to the side of the road, along with the vehicle you clobbered. Car number two, the one that skillfully distracted you, is long gone. As the fellow you hit gets out of his car, you see that he's holding his neck and wincing in pain, and you begin to get a sinking sensation. But being a good citizen, you inquire about his injury and dutifully pull out your driver's license. Although the "injured party" is quick to copy down pertinent information about you and your insurance company, he has difficulty responding to *your* questions. It seems that his old clunker is uninsured, and his agony appears to increase by the moment. As you stand there watching traffic whiz by, you wonder how you got so unlucky.

Days later, your insurer receives a claim from the injured party, who by this time has secured an attorney and an alarming prognosis from a cooperative doctor or chiropractor, and you find yourself at the wrong end of a lawsuit. At the very least, the "accident" will go on your record and your insurance rates will soar. Although you'll undoubtedly undergo a significant amount of stress, there will be no compensation for *your* suffering.

How can you avoid this kind of scam? The old adage about an ounce of prevention immediately comes to mind. When you're on the road, be on the lookout for any vehicle that seems to be hovering right in front of you. If you make an effort not to tailgate and still find yourself too close for comfort, change lanes! If the suspicious car moves over too and repositions itself in front of you, warning bells should go off.

At that point, if another driver is making a bid for your attention, ignore him and, if necessary, pull off the road or exit the freeway as quickly as possible. Make it clear by your definitive actions that you're not going to be suckered into any kind of situation.

But if such a setup occurs too quickly for you to avoid it, here's the best thing to do:

- Don't give the "injured" driver your driver's license number and bid him adieu.
- Insist on summoning the police.
- Try to locate witnesses.

This may be enough to discourage the scamster. If not, when an officer arrives, tell him or her exactly what happened and provide as clear a description as possible of the second car, recalling, if you can, make, model, color, and the appearance of the driver. Your actions alone might scare the scam artist into having second thoughts. If you can document your case effectively, you might not only save yourself from legal action but also help catch a con artist.

LEASING SCAMS

To buy or not to buy? The advantages of leasing a car over outright purchase depend on the use of the vehicle and the your or your company's tax situation. In many instances leasing is suggested by accountants as the best way to go.

But beware of any leasing situation that doesn't proceed strictly by the book, especially if you're told not to worry about financing. Those whose shaky credit ratings prevent them from acquiring a bank loan sometimes end up with a leasing company that assures them that qualifying will be "no problem." After signing papers and agreeing to a high rate of interest, the happy customer drives home in a new car. He is understandably upset if, a short time later, the leasing company suddenly closes up shop, leaving him to deal with a bank that won't accept his credit.

Some shady leasing companies issue front money to individuals who purchase vehicles for the firm in their own names. Sometimes these cars are then leased to customers who don't want the automobiles traced (drug dealers come to mind) or to people with weak credit who can't qualify for a loan through normal channels. What some of these third parties don't know is that unless their lease agreement receives the consent of the bank, it is against the law. When banks discover that unqualified persons are driving these vehicles, they can recall the cars or press charges or both.

If you lease a vehicle from a well-established company, you have little cause for worry. But if you deal with an unfamiliar firm, especially one that offers you credit when others have refused, ask to see *all* the paperwork. You don't want to participate, even unwittingly, in any kind of double-dealing. Or one way or another you'll end up paying far more than you bargained for.

Burglars Who Pose as Valet Parkers

A young executive returned to his luxury condo one evening with friends in tow, for a cappuccino nightcap. As he ushered his pals into his sunken living room, he gasped. His stereo equipment and VCR were missing. A quick check of the other rooms proved equally alarming. His computer and fax machine were nowhere in sight. In all, his estimated loss ran into the thousands. And the most disturbing thing was that there was no sign of forced entry. It appeared that not a window or a door had been touched.

When the police questioned the stunned victim about friends or relatives who might have keys to his home, the young man agonized. His trusted housekeeper had a key, and so did, possibly, a former roommate. But it distressed him to think that someone close could have been involved in such a vile act. "Think hard," said the officer. "Have you handed your key out to any strangers? How about repairmen? Valet attendants?"

Uh-oh! Two nights before he had taken a date to his favorite restaurant. As he slowed his car to look for a parking place, an attractive young woman in slacks, hat, and a matching vest ran up and opened his door. "Hi, My name's Jan! We're starting a new valet service and this is your lucky night 'cause tonight's on the house." Charmed by the young woman's smile and demeanor, and happy to find free parking, he quickly handed over his key ring.

One call to the restaurant confirmed the worst. The management had no knowledge of a valet service whose attendants sported red uniforms and gold name tags. It had definitely not been this young exec's lucky night after all, for the keys he handed over included one to the door of his apartment.

Such clever operations are not uncommon, nor are they new. Yet people who are revved up for an evening out often don't stop to observe the strangers with whom they're entrusting their car, their keys, and, ultimately, all their possessions. This con game is simple enough: While you are dining, the "valet" takes your keys to a nearby garage where he has a key-making device on hand. He makes a duplicate, then easily locates your address in the glove compartment or on the car registration.

Here are a few ways to make sure you don't unwittingly grant someone entrance to your humble home or castle:

• Always carry a spare set of car keys to give to mechanics and valets. Give them *only* the car key.
• Look twice at parking attendants before you hand over your car and keys. If it's not a service you're familiar with, check with the maître d' or other personnel of the establishment being served.

GOOD SAMARITAN "MECHANICS"

Cathy was sailing through a Saturday of shopping and errands, racing to get home and prepare for her dinner guests. Throwing her packages in the trunk, she jumped in her car, turned the ignition key and—nothing. As the engine turned over and the dash lights flashed on, she held her breath, but in vain. Ready to scream, she was heartened when a nice-looking man strolled by and offered, "I think it might be your computer."

The man smiled, explained that he was a mechanic, and told Cathy that if the car's computer, which controlled the fuel pump, was on the blink, her engine wouldn't be getting any gas. If she was in a hurry he thought he could get her a new one for maybe $100. When Cathy hesitated, Sir Galahad said he thought he might be able to fix it. Pulling out his trusty screwdriver, he fooled around under the dash for a couple of minutes, then told the frustrated driver to try again. The engine purred, and Cathy was back in business.

But, gosh, how could she ever thank him?

The knight-with-a-knack shuffled his feet and mumbled something about a "few dollars for gas," at which point the grateful lady gave him $20 and sped happily away. Chivalry wasn't dead.

But that night at dinner, as she relayed her story to her guests, a friend gave her reason to pause. "The computer doesn't control the fuel pump," he told her. "But there's a connector near the gas tank in late-model cars. If it's disconnected, your pump won't work."

Do these connectors come unplugged all by themselves? Not likely. The chances are that Cathy's benefactor, working with a sidekick, unplugged the connector while she was in the store. And when she refused his offer to help her buy a new computer, while the "mechanic" held her attention fiddling around under the dash, his accomplice fixed the connector.

It's an old trick, with lots of variations. The next time someone pops up at a crucial moment with advice that can cost you, say no thanks and call your auto club or a reputable mechanic. Or check the connector yourself. Just be sure you send Sir Galahad on his way, empty-handed.

Slick Car Dealers

Car salespersons rank somewhere in the depths of the public's collective consciousness, along with such perceived bottom dwellers as attorneys, politicians, and members of the media. But in spite of this wariness, we still hear reports of customers getting taken in by slick dealers.

Price variances are probably the most dicey area for prospective car buyers. But instead of being a liability, they can actually work *for* the buyer who knows what he or she is doing. Unlike department store merchandise, auto prices are notoriously flexible. Getting the best possible deal depends on your haggling skills, since purchasing a car often boils down to a battle of wits between the customer and the salesperson.

The question for many consumers is how to begin bidding. Just like at auctions, there has to be a starting price. Some say a good rule of thumb is to take $3,000 off the sticker price and then subtract the dealer's prep charge. That's your opening offer.

After you've made your bold first bid, you'll no doubt be escorted into the famous back room where deals are made. Although rumors of bare lightbulbs and food deprivation are greatly exaggerated, this is not the time or place to let down your guard.

Your salesperson will sit down and begin poring over figures at the computer terminal. Think of him as the "good cop." In the midst of his ruminations, his evil twin (the sales manager) will make his entrance. Together they'll conspire and eventually arrive at a counteroffer.

If their figure isn't even in the ballpark of your quote, take a deep breath, whisper a prayer or your favorite mantra, and add no more than $500 to your bid. And then make a quick exit, right out the door like a bunny, before they have a chance to work you over.

With any luck, your salesperson will call you the next day with a lower price. The point is, however skilled or unskilled a poker player you may be, *never* close a deal on day one. Bite your tongue. The longer you haggle, the longer you hold out, the more favorable the deal will be for you.

If you're nervous about being outnumbered or outsmarted in the back room, it might help your morale and your actual presentation to be accompanied by a friend. If you have an acquaintance who is in the car business, or a pal who happens to resemble Marlon Brando's character in *The Godfather,* so much the better. Think of it as a game and play to win. No matter what the outcome of your bidding war, you are certain to get your car at a better price than if you walk in and offer no resistance to the sticker price.

Other points to keep in mind: Don't let the dealer compensate for your low purchase price by offering too little for your trade-in. You might do better selling it yourself. And beware of "extended warranties." Whether you're buying a washing machine or a car, these extra warranties are usually of little benefit, except as a money-making gimmick for the company.

Scam Artists Who "Steal" Your Good Driving Record

A former California highway patrolman who teaches traffic school in Los Angeles warns his students about more than just the hazards of speeding. He tells his class that if they care about having a clean driving record, they'd best request a copy from the Department of Motor Vehicles once or twice a year. It seems that it's possible to get a citation for an accident or drunk driving even while you're home in bed!

The way it works is this: An errant driver who has one or two driving-under-the-influence convictions or outstanding warrants knows that one more incident will probably land him in jail. Not a pretty thought. So some of these scamsters keep their eyes out for another driver's license number to use in place of their own.

All this person needs is a job as a cashier, or a friend or relative who checks license numbers as a form of ID. When someone is spotted who resembles the wayward driver in age and physical description, the bad guy zeros in. Because he doesn't want to assume the identity of a serial killer, he makes sure the person whose ID he's "borrowing" looks super straight, the kind of person who probably has a clean driving record.

The next time the delinquent driver goes out drinking and has one too many for the road, he doesn't worry about the flashing red lights in his rearview mirror. When he's pulled over, he explains to the officer that his license is at home. "But," he says with a cooperative smile, "I know my number by heart." The trouble is, the number he recites may be *yours!*

Your first inkling that you're now a wanted man or woman may come in the form of a bench warrant or letter of cancellation from your insurance company. At that point you have no choice but to take quick action, which may require hiring an attorney. There's no way to ensure against such a travesty other than to hand your license number out as infrequently as possible by using cash or credit cards in place of checks. And as the traffic school cop recommends, request a copy of your driving record from time to time so you can clear up any errors before someone comes looking for you with a pair of handcuffs.

Used Cars with "Laundered" Titles

A Detroit man recently bought a used car for his son to take to college. He thought he got a great deal. The auctioned vehicle looked good, handled well, and had low mileage. When he asked whether the car had ever been in an accident, the answer was, "Nothing serious."

But before the son's first semester was half over, he no longer had wheels. His new used car died an ignoble death on the way to a sorority picnic. Upset by the unlikely turn of events, the father did some checking and found that the car's history included a high-speed head-on collision.

At this time, obscure loopholes in certain states make it possible for motor vehicle records to be altered. Because there are no universal standards to govern classifications, scam artists as well as car thieves can "wash" negative input such as "wreck" or "salvage" off titles, leaving the cars with an apparently clean bill of health. In other cases, a lack of consistent definitions is the problem. Some states consider a vehicle to be a "wreck" if only a few parts need replacement, while others require that a repair bill total greater than 80 percent of the car's value before being so categorized.

The bottom line is that this practice costs consumers an estimated $4 billion a year. In individual cases, the damage varies. While some mislabeled cars rattle on in spite of their checkered pasts, many of them are world-class lemons. A federal commission is currently studying ways to make title labeling more uniform.

How Not to Advertise Your Used Car

A Miami woman recently advertised her slightly used Toyota Camry in a local paper. Among interested callers was a representative from an outfit claiming to match automobile buyers and sellers. "Some of our buyers are willing to pay more than the asking price," said the man on the phone, "if it's the right car."

When the woman asked what it would cost to list with his agency, he replied, "It won't cost you a cent unless we get you a buyer." It sounded as if there was nothing to lose, and with a nothing-ventured-nothing-gained mindset, the woman replied, "Sign me up."

A few days later she received a call from the same man, saying, "We've got a live one!" The live one, it seemed, was willing to pay $3,000 more than her asking price.

"Why has he agreed to pay so much?" the woman wisely asked.

"He's been looking for a silver Camry, blue upholstery, stereo, all the extras. Your car is exactly what he wants, and he has to leave for Europe next week. Time is money."

It sounded reasonable, so when the man requested a "search fee" of $200 before giving out the referral, the woman agreed and mailed in her check. When a week passed and no buyer was forthcoming, she called the agency and was told, "This guy had to leave town sooner than he expected, but we're getting another buyer lined up."

But more time went by and the agency still didn't deliver the goods. When the woman requested a refund, she was given the royal runaround.

Other companies of this type sometimes offer a computer search with an (almost) money-back guarantee. For example, they may ask for $220, with the provision that if a car isn't sold in ninety days, they'll refund $200 and keep $20 for processing costs. This isn't a bad deal for the company. While they're holding your cash, they can earn quarterly interest, plus the $20. They're guaranteed to make money whether a car is ever sold or not.

If you're considering signing up with any kind of matchmaking agency, don't be in a rush. Check out the company first with the Better Business Bureau. If you have any question at all, it's best to stick with classified advertising in a local paper or a publication like *Auto Trader* that specializes in car sales.

Phony Companies That Want to Buy Your Car

As if enough grief doesn't result from natural disasters, there are always scam artists who see an angle in every fiasco. Recently a man in a flood-stricken area advertised his Ford Bronco in the classified section of his local newspaper. One of his first callers was a woman who identified herself as an agent with a prominent insurance firm.

After initial pleasantries, she explained, "Our company's trying to replace cars that were lost or ruined in the flood. Let me tell you, it's a big job!" Then she asked for details about his Bronco's condition and mileage and made what the man considered to be a fair offer. When they reached an agreement, she said, "I'll need an address where it can be picked up and your checking account number so we can make a direct deposit to your bank."

Of course, no one came to claim the car, and instead of a deposit, the man found that someone had attempted to withdraw money from his account. When taking calls on a vehicle ad, always insist on a cashier's check, whether the buyer is an individual or a company. Don't let the "legitimacy" of a big firm throw you — or take you.

Dealers Who Sell Your Trade-In and Leave You Carless

After years of hard work, a Portland woman was made vice president of her firm, and along with her promotion came a hefty raise. She decided to celebrate with a new car. No longer in the ranks of those who must drive a previously owned vehicle, she was thrilled when she walked into a showroom and spotted a sleek ice-blue sports car.

Because she was just entering a new salary range, the woman was concerned about financing, but the avuncular sales manager smiled and said not to worry. "Go ahead and take the car home," he urged. "I'll call you as soon as the loan's been arranged. All I need is a down payment, say a thousand or two, and your trade-in, and you can drive this baby out of here."

The new VP couldn't ask for more than that. She raced home in her glorious new car and proudly showed it off to her family and friends. Everyone agreed it was the perfect auto for her new station in life.

After two days of four-wheeled bliss, the sales manager called and told the owner that her credit had been turned down. Her spirits and self-esteem took a nosedive. What would she tell people when she returned the blue beauty and reclaimed her tired old Chevy?

It turned out she needn't have worried about the latter situation. "You know what?" the salesman said, "Right after you left here a young kid came in and couldn't wait to get his hands on your old car. His family had all chipped in and given him cash for his birthday, so he took it on the spot. We didn't even have time to wash it."

The woman's heart dropped one notch lower. It appeared she was without a car. She couldn't afford her new one, and her old one was gone. She envisioned herself being her company's first vice president to take the bus.

"Don't worry, honey," soothed the sales manager in his best I'm-coming-to-the-rescue voice. "I'm not going to let you wear out your shoes. If you put down another two grand I think I can swing a smaller loan."

"That's a lot of money."

"Well, then maybe instead of the deluxe model I could let you have one without the extras." The woman pictured herself driving to work with a tape player on the seat, while she sweated on plastic seat covers.

Feeling that she was in an untenable situation, the woman finally said, "I guess I can tap my savings."

What she didn't know was that she had not forfeited her old car. Sold or not, the dealer was bound by law to get the trade-in car back, if so requested. Otherwise, he would have to pay the value of the car, plus damages. Second, the dealer had no right to keep any part of his customer's down payment, even if she chose to take her business elsewhere.

Never allow yourself to be pressured by strong-arm tactics. If a credit situation isn't to your liking, you have the right to get your old car back and to shop around for another loan and/or for other car dealers.

7

TAKING CHANCES—
CONTESTS,
SALES, AND
PROMOTIONS

It's a rare person who's never fantasized about winning the lottery. And even those who rarely gamble will once in a while put a stamp on an envelope or enter their name in a drawing with the rationalization that there's nothing to lose. While that may be technically true, keep in mind that contests are never run for the benefit of the participants. Before trying for the brass ring, it's wise to consider what the backers of the contest stand to gain—at your expense.

WRITING "CONTESTS"

While they may not be easily swayed by the promise of riches, aspiring writers and artists are particularly susceptible to the lure of limelight. One perfectly legal but shameless operation involves certain writing and poetry contests. Cash prizes are usually awarded to the winners, and those who receive honorable mention get to have their work published in a leather-bound anthology. To anyone who's never seen his or her name in print, this sounds like an attractive proposition. If there's a modest fee to enter the contest, most participants are willing to pay. The catch here is that contests of this type are merely a clever device for selling books.

Lars Eighner, who wrote so poignantly about his three years of homelessness in the book *Travels with Lisbeth,* tells of a down-on-his-luck acquaintance who fancied himself a poet. On learning about a national poetry contest, this man entered three of his best poems. The author warned him of the contest's true agenda, but the poet was intent on pursuing his dreams. Sure enough, just as Eighner predicted, the fellow didn't end up in the winner's circle, but two of his three poems won honorable mention and would thus be included in the anthology.

Thrilled with his "success," the indigent poet couldn't wait to get his hands on a copy of this esteemed tome to show his cronies that he was, indeed, a published poet. The homeless man sacrificed and somehow managed to raise the hefty fee for one copy of the book. When it arrived, leather-bound and impressively turned out, he was thrilled to see his work in print and oblivious to the fact that the publishers were making an astronomical profit.

But the story doesn't end there. Not long after this drifter received his book, another letter arrived at his mailing address. More incredible news! His third poem, the one that hadn't made honorable mention, was going to be included in an anthology for "special" works. The honor of possessing this second volume would, of course, require another sizable check. In spite of Eighner's continued admonitions, the novice poet again made painful sacrifices to come up with the fee. And when he received his second book and bragged to his friends about his accomplishments, a couple of his pals found themselves bitten by the bug. Soon they too entered their poetry in a subsequent contest. And they, like their friend, paid handsomely for their vanity.

For those who can afford the luxury of being self-published, there's no harm done. But these types of books are sold only to the contributors and are not placed in mainstream distribution. For the same amount of money, you could have your own book of poems printed, without having to share the glory with other anonymous and possibly abominable authors.

THE HIDDEN COST OF ENTERING "FREE" DRAWINGS

Here's the scenario: A stranger calls just as you're finishing dinner and tells you she's conducting a marketing survey and needs two minutes of your time. All she wants to know is your name, address (she already has your phone number), age, gender and . . . income. No way, José. She's history. Even when a preppy-looking young man stops you in the mall and asks for your assistance in some market research he's doing, you're probably inclined to give him the brush-off.

But if you happen to be racing through a supermarket or shopping center and see a shiny new red convertible with a sign reading "Win Me!" you may screech to a halt. You read the entry rules or listen to a spiel from an attractive hostess. Hey, there's nothing to buy, no fee to pay, no other contest to enter. Just put your name on the entry blank and drop it in the slot.

Of course there's a line on the form that reads: "Please fill out completely." But it's only a few questions: addresses, telephone number, age, sex, family income—the same information you refused to give the caller on the phone.

But it seems fair enough to ask those questions of someone who might receive a spiffy new car. So you take half a minute, toss your form in the box, and briefly fantasize about sailing down the highway with the wind in your hair. If the contest allows you to enter more than once you might even throw in a couple more entry blanks, just to give fate a helping hand.

Sounds like a good deal. This is one contest that's virtually risk free. You don't have to buy or subscribe to anything, so there's absolutely nothing to lose. But the caveat here is what you might have to gain—junk mail!

Companies that buy and sell mailing lists are big business. Entrepreneurs of all kinds pay top dollar for lists of persons and households who represent their target audience. Consequently, enterprising individuals can make a good living selling these lists to marketing firms.

But how do they acquire thousands of names with current addresses? They know that soliciting people in person or over the phone doesn't work very well. But contests have proven to be an easy way to collect names.

The cost of the prize car is a fraction of what can be made by selling the up-to-date information that results.

If more information is desired, follow-up phone calls are made to contest participants, informing them that they are now finalists! With such good news, people are likely to donate a minute of their time and even report spending preferences.

If you're into long shots, there's no reason not to try and win that terrific sports car. But know that you might find yourself the recipient of unwanted junk mail for a long time to come. You could try outfoxing them by stating on the form that you're unemployed or below the poverty line, or simply provide no information other than your name and phone number. Of course if you do that, you probably won't win. But you probably wouldn't have won anyway.

Why You Shouldn't Call to Collect Your Grand Prize

Beware of winning contests you never entered. Marketing firms often send out "prize confirmation" notices informing "winners" that they've just been awarded a free trip (which probably doesn't include transportation) or some other supposedly valuable prize. But before you can receive this terrific gift, you need to confirm your eligibility. You're given a telephone number to call, usually a 900 line, which at $3 or $4 a minute will wind up costing more than a few bucks by the time you're through.

Even if you're given an 800 number to call, you should still be skeptical. Some outfits have the 800 number forwarded to a 900 number, in which case you won't realize you've been charged until your next phone bill rolls in.

Sometimes you're informed, either by phone or mail, that you have definitely won one of several prizes. The list may include a new car, an exotic cruise, a costly appliance such as a computer or camcorder, or a diamond ring. There's usually some reasonable-sounding fee that you must pay to qualify. The catch here is that the overwhelming majority of lucky "winners" receive the diamond ring. Worth how much? Well, they didn't say exactly how large the diamond was, so when you receive a cheap trinket sporting the world's tiniest (alleged) diamond chip, you'll probably just shrug it off and give the "prize" to your favorite niece. Meanwhile, the contest executives deposit your money in the bank.

Remember, a genuine prize should be a gift—free, with absolutely no strings attached!

THE "GOVERNMENT AGENT" SCAM

Just like the phony car mechanic who disables a vehicle and then offers to fix it for small fee, contest con artists sometimes operate the same way. A Denver couple was taken in by a telemarketing scheme that promised them a new car if they would buy one of several appliances offered by the company. Because they had been shopping for just such a product, they jumped at the chance to win a new car while making a necessary purchase.

But their appliance, when it finally arrived, was of such poor quality that it soon had to be replaced. And the big prize—the car? In their dreams. When they called the company to complain to the "nice gentleman" who first notified them of their windfall, they reached a disconnected number.

Embarrassed by their naïveté, they decided to put the matter behind them and consider it an expensive lesson. But a few weeks later they received a call from a "government agent" who claimed to be conducting an investigation. He told the couple that they were on a list of consumers who had been victimized by this particular telephone fraud. And with the help of all those who had lost money, the scamsters would soon be derailed.

The couple received some official-looking paperwork, which they filled out, and sent along a processing fee of $100. Guess what? That money went into the same pockets as their first payout, for the "fraud squad" agent was in cahoots with the original swindlers. In their desire to even the score, the good guys struck out twice and the bad guys won again.

If you are ever approached by someone from the police department or any government agency, ask to see more than his or her badge. Call the bureau he or she is allegedly working for, as well as the National Fraud

Information Center at (800) 876-7060, to double-check. It's the only way
to avoid double trouble.

Clubs That Trick You into Joining

A budget-conscious career woman received a postcard in the mail offering her a free product. She usually tossed such mail in the wastebasket,
but after reading the text carefully, she was convinced that all she had to
do was return the card and receive her gift.

Several weeks later she received not one, but three items in the mail,
along with a bill for the second and third pair, plus shipping and handling charges. The invoice also stated that she was now enrolled in a club,
similar to a book- or record-of-the-month club. Unless she notified the
company otherwise, would receive a shipment every few weeks. Annoyed
at the tricky ploy, the woman promptly sent back all three items and insisted that her name be removed from their list of "club members."

The old saying "there's no such thing as a free lunch" rings true. Beware of "free" gifts that may obligate you to purchase unwanted merchandise, be it books, records, or any other products.

Slick Salesmen Who Take Advantage of Customer Greed

There's the New Yorker who walked into a furniture showroom during
a big sale and found the place nearly empty. "Not much business, huh?"
he said sympathetically to the manager.

After the obligatory "business is great" spiel, the manager glumly ad-
mitted, "Bad time of year, I guess."

"For $5,000 I can promise to sell everything in this store in one day,"
said the man.

"Oh sure."

"You don't owe me a cent until I've cleared the place out."

"And if not, I don't owe you anything?"

"Not a penny."

The skeptical sales manager figured he had nothing to lose. He hired
the man to come in and work the floor the following Saturday.

The day came, and customers wandered in. The new salesman would approach them and ask, "Which piece are you interested in?" If they indicated a sofa, he'd call to the manager upstairs, "Hey, Charlie, what's the lowest we can go on this?"

The manager, as instructed, would call down the prearranged price of $900.

Then the temporary salesman would fiddle around with a conspicuously large hearing aid and holler again, "How much?"

"Nine hundred!"

At this point he would shake his head and tell the customer, "I think he said five hundred."

The sofa sold on the spot, as did every item on the floor. By the end of the day the man had made good on his promise. The old "something-for-nothing ploy," often the tool of scam artists, seems to have eternal appeal.

All retailers mark up their wares. And there's no way to know the actual value of a given item. But if you think you're getting a "deal" at someone else's expense, you might be getting less than you think.

8

TELEPHONE
TREACHERY

Long ago and far away, in an era most of us have forgotten or never knew, one could pick up the telephone receiver and hear a voice say, "Number please." The caller would then recite the number he or she wished to reach, and a real live operator would place the call.

Oh, how far we've come! Now we punch in our numbers on a touch-tone phone (sometimes as many as twenty-four digits, when we're making a credit-card call), and we're immediately connected with the Voicemail of our choice. Or we can punch in a pager number and disturb whomever we wish, who, if he or she so desires, can "get right back to us." With cellular phones we can reach out and touch someone at 80 miles per hour, or simply reach into our pocket and make electronic contact at any moment of the night or day.

But all this technology that has made our lives simpler — or more complicated, as the case may be — also has made the lives of scam artists easier. Those who specialize in rip-offs now have millions of potential victims literally at their fingertips.

How 900 Numbers "Steal" Your Money

The 900 numbers used to be associated solely with adult entertainment. But the menu has expanded to include a deluge of information lines, some of them quite legitimate, others more questionable. While these advertised numbers generally provide the information their callers seek, many are contrived to stretch out the call (and the cost) as long as possible.

Let's say, for example, that you've heard about the great deals at government auctions. Maybe you need a new car, or office equipment such as a copier or computer. You've heard on the radio or read in the newspapers about a 900 number that notifies the caller of locations of upcoming auctions and provides tips on how to bid successfully.

In fine print or at the end of a radio commercial, you are informed of the cost of the call, perhaps $2 or $3 per minute. You figure it's worth it because you'll be able to save a bundle on the merchandise you're going to buy. So you dial the number and are greeted by a cheerful voice welcoming you to the information line. The voice states that at the end of the message you'll hear a list of auctions, complete with time, date, and location. That's the meat of the message and the payoff for the few dollars you expect to pay.

However, before you get to the "beef," the meter starts ticking away. After a record-breaking greeting, you may be told in glowing terms about all the benefits of purchasing goods at auction prices. You can, the voice suggests, buy items at below-the-line prices and then resell them for a quick profit, thus generating a second income without quitting your present job. Once again you're promised that at the end of the message you'll receive a list of when and where the auctions will be held.

As you glance at your watch, waiting impatiently for them to cut to the chase, the disembodied voice drones on about how much you're going to enjoy your newfound fortune. Just think of the wardrobe, the Hawaiian vacations, and exciting new lifestyle that can be yours if you become an auction wheeler-dealer!

The trouble is, as you sit there with the phone at your ear, a truly captive audience, the minutes keep ticking away. Surely *now* the voice will kindly give you the information that prompted you to dial. But wait a moment—not only can you use your extra income for luxuries, if you're smart and motivated, you can parlay this money into financial independence! Just think, retirement at an early age, more time to spend with your loved ones. . . .

After all this useless gab, you're so annoyed you consider hanging up. But common sense tells you that you're not the one who will have the last laugh. By now they've gotten so many of your dollars without relinquishing any real information that you're in a bind. If you hang up you'll have spent all that money in vain. Like a loser at the racetrack, you can't afford to quit, so you hang in there, hoping that your persistence will finally be rewarded.

And eventually, after all the rhetoric, here comes the message. For a special amazing price you can buy a book or tape telling you more about the auction business. Now you must listen to a spiel hyping this product, with more verbosity about how rich you're going to be.

Finally, just as you're ready to verbally assault the recorded voice, it rattles off the pertinent information. But wait! In your hurry to jot down the vital statistics, your pen runs out of ink and . . . Now you'll have to hang up and start all over again!

While you'll ultimately receive the advertised information—which is usually quite valid—the scam here is that instead of receiving your details immediately, at the cost of a couple of dollars, 900 numbers often string out the call for several minutes, and that can add up to $10 to $20, depending on the number you call and the charge per minute.

900 Numbers That Prey on Kids

A busy mother received an unwelcome surprise when she glanced over her monthly phone bill. The total was almost $100 higher than usual. On closer inspection she saw that the extra dollars were the result of numerous 900 calls, all to the same number. After confirming that these extra charges were not her husband's doing, she braced herself for the worst-case scenario. Their thirteen-year-old son must have been calling one of those sexually oriented phone lines. The frantic mother insisted that her spouse sit down with the boy and embark on a serious father-son discussion.

On questioning his son about the unauthorized calls, the dad warned him about the dangers of everything from dishonesty to cheap vicarious thrills. The boy, with all the wisdom of his thirteen years, said, "Dad, I don't know what you're talking about. Why don't you just dial the number and see what you get?"

Chagrined at not having checked out the number before making accusations, the distressed dad dialed the 900 number and was greeted by a squeaky and decidedly unsexy voice. Some cartoonlike character carried on an inane monologue for several minutes, then urged him to "be sure and call again tomorrow."

It turned out to be the couple's younger son who was the telephone offender. Apparently the precocious six-year-old had been responding to a compelling ad on afternoon TV. The little one had been enticed into calling a number that would allow him to "talk" to his favorite furry character. It wasn't much of a conversation, however, just a one-sided babble that kept the meter ticking away and concluded with instructions to call again. And again.

The dad and his son did have a heart-to-heart about the facts of life, and the result was successful. The first-grader learned that telephone calls cost money and should never be made without permission. This kind of communication can never begin too early in life.

WHY LOCAL LONG-DISTANCE COMPANIES ARE DANGEROUS TO YOUR (FINANCIAL) HEALTH

If E.T. had been able to call home, he might have been in for a shock. Most of us have seen or heard ads giving numbers for accessing AT&T or MCI, or watched a radiant Candice Bergen proclaiming the virtues of Sprint, and thought all phone companies are pretty much the same. Right?

Wrong. That may be true among the major competitors. And I'm not here to debate the benefits of AT&T over MCI or Sprint or vice versa. When it comes to long-distance dialing, it's the little guys you have to watch out for.

A woman was vacationing at a ski resort one Christmas and had to make frequent business calls to keep in touch with her clients. When she punched in her calling card number, a pleasant female voice came briefly on the line, saying, "Thank you for using . . ." The caller didn't recognize the name of the obscure phone company but assumed that even if they charged a few cents more than her regular long-distance company, it was no big deal. It was a business expense, and she could write it off. Anxious to get back to the slopes, she didn't feel like going through the hassle of punching in still more numbers in an effort to access AT&T.

But weeks later when she received her phone bill, she was in for a surprise. It seems the little long-distance company that had so merrily thanked her for her business was making out like a bandit. In place of a small surcharge on each call, the woman was billed $1 to $2 for each and every minute she was on the line! In all, this otherwise savvy businesswoman found that her impatience had cost her a couple of hundred dollars!

The moral here is to take that extra minute and access your regular long-distance company. Whichever one you've decided to use is sure to cost you less than the local companies that make you pay through the nose for a moment of convenience.

THE SLAMMING SCAM

Slamming may sound like something you'd do on the dance floor, but actually it's another telephone scam, also involving obscure and expensive long-distance companies. One Philadelphia woman who believed she was using AT&T began to notice a time lag when she called other states; sometimes it took the better part of a minute before her calls went through. And while she waited she was treated to a number of loud and annoying beeps.

But that was nothing compared to her annoyance when she received her next phone bill! Her service had been transferred to a long-distance carrier she'd never heard of, whose charges were more than double those of AT&T.

Normally, if you want to change long-distance companies, you contact the new company and have them make the arrangements. But the system has its flaws. The term "slamming" is used to describe the aggressive techniques of small phone companies that increase their business by literally hijacking new accounts. Some of these firms send out contest entries where your signature actually authorizes a switch from your company to theirs. (This is stated in *very* fine print.) Or they send out small ($10 to $20) checks during promotional campaigns. Again, the small print reveals that cashing the check authorizes them to become your new long-distance carrier.

In some instances, accounts are successfully hijacked without using either of these ruses. In these cases names are simply chosen at random. Often, the selected "customers" have foreign surnames, for these companies do best by targeting immigrants who may have difficulty with English, especially when the words appear in letters the size of microbes.

If you find yourself a prisoner of a long-distance company you've never heard of, contact your previous company, explain what happened, and ask to be switched back and have your billing adjusted. And when you get anything in the mail that's not from your mother, read the fine print!

Avoid Paying a Fortune When Calling from Overseas

Speaking of convenience, the farther from home you go, the more you pay for it. In foreign countries, travelers often are warned not to place overseas calls from their hotel rooms. With the hotel's surcharge, the cost of a call can easily double.

Some foreign hotels now belong to Tele-Plan, a program that keeps telephone charges down to a reasonable level. It's a good idea to check before dialing out. And if you feel that thriftiness is next to godliness, the smartest way of all to reach out and touch someone when you're abroad is to go to the local phone company. These offices are often adjoining the post office, and the clerks there will place your call directly, so you'll be charged only the basic fee.

INVOICE "CLONES"

There are many ways to advertise a business, but the good old Yellow Pages offers reasonable rates for broad circulation. Many entrepreneurs and independent contractors select the phone book as their primary and sometimes only form of promotion.

In a recent newsletter, Pacific Bell Smart Yellow Pages issued a warning to its customers. Some unethical firms had been creating clever pieces of sales material that looked like invoices for Yellow Pages advertising. And experts figured that at least one in fifty of these Yellow Pages invoice "clones" prompted payments from confused and busy customers.

According to Pacific Bell, these fake bills can be spotted in three ways:

- The words "THIS IS NOT A BILL" must appear on all solicitations. Be sure to scan any invoice you're uncertain about for this declaration.
- All real invoices include a telephone number of a representative you can call with questions. If you receive a "bill" that has no number, it's bogus.
- Yellow Pages invoices rarely exceed $150 a month, so beware of "bills" for larger amounts.

PROTECT YOUR TELEPHONE CALLING-CARD NUMBER

A busy reporter gets off a plane in Atlanta and, juggling his laptop and overnight bag, makes his way to a pay phone. He punches in his phone company calling-card number and rings his editor in Washington. It's a routine call and he thinks no more about it until a few weeks later when he receives a record-shattering phone bill.

Someone had gotten hold of his card number and, within a few hours, had run up thousands of dollars of long-distance costs. Because his card had never been lost or stolen, it's likely that this man was victimized by a "shoulder surfer" in the crowded airport. These people watch callers punch in their numbers, either by looking directly over their shoulders or watching from a distance with binoculars. Some use a pen and notepad, but many recite numbers into microphones hidden in their sleeves. Still others waltz by with a camcorder and videotape callers at the vital moment.

Then they put the stolen number to work. Some sell their "goods" to middlemen who then market the numbers on the street. In cities that are home to large numbers of immigrants, there is always a steady stream of customers without phones who want to call home. A "button man" takes cash from a line of foreigners who queue up to talk to Mama or the girl back home. Let's just say, for example, that he rakes in $20 for each three-minute call. That's about $400 an hour, a rate that's likely to make even a few attorneys pale with envy!

The moral here is that when dialing from a public phone, never assume you're alone. Be aware of anyone hovering nearby, and if you see someone playing Steven Spielberg with a video camera, make sure it's not pointing at you when you press the buttons.

AIDS Information: You Shouldn't Have to Pay for It

Another legal scam involving 900 numbers is a cruel one because it targets those suffering from AIDS. Flyers are faxed to individuals and organizations, urging them to call a 900 number for the latest AIDS research data. Sometimes the sheet states that all proceeds will go to such-and-such AIDS research project, often an organization no one has heard of.

Although the information provided may be factual, it can also be outdated, and it is definitely costly at $5 or so per minute. A printed transcript may also be offered for an additional charge.

If you wish the latest data on AIDS or any other medical research, call major research centers or hospitals in your area. For information on clinical trials, call (800) TRIALS-A or (800) HIV-0440 for data on federally approved treatments. There is no charge for these services.

9

Investment

and

Financial

Scams

Of all the scams floating around, those that appeal to that old devil greed are among the most ubiquitous and successful. It's a rare person who couldn't use some extra cash, and "deals" that offer a quick and/or hefty return on our dollar are eternally appealing. And it's not just poor or uneducated individuals who are susceptible. Some of the most notorious schemes are specially targeted at the rich and famous. So before you write a check to any outfit you're not absolutely sure about, think twice. And do your homework.

When Not to Pay Loan Fees

There's always a market for those in need of loans, and the numbers soar during hard times. Whenever there's a recession resulting in unemployment and damaged credit, there's a plethora of ads offering "personal loans." These ads are usually in the classified section and offer thousands of dollars in available cash. The only stipulation is that the applicant pay an up-front fee of a few hundred dollars to cover the cost of "processing."

While some of these advertisements are legitimate, there are fly-by-night operations in which the applicant hands over the fee and never sees the promised cash. Before you write a check to anyone who advertises in the paper, inquire about the company through the Better Business Bureau and make sure the operation is on the level. Loan fees should always come out of the loan itself and never be paid in advance.

$\textit{B}$ogus $\mathscr{A}$rt

Paintings can be a lucrative investment and a lot more fun than stocks and bonds because you can hang them on your wall. Knowledgeable collectors have profited handsomely from selected works of art that appreciate at a higher rate than the Dow Jones industrials. While experienced art buyers may be hard to fool, vacationers who wander through galleries in upscale tourist spots are easy marks for retailers selling bogus paintings. Smooth-talking dealers present "original" prints by famous artists, convincing prospective buyers that the works are rare and therefore a great investment. If a patron appears skeptical and arm-twisting is necessary, certificates of authenticity are on hand to clinch the deal.

Such bogus prints are often sold for prices ranging from a thousand dollars up into the tens of thousands. In place of genuine limited-edition prints that are manually pulled off the press and signed by the artist, photo reproductions with a retail value of no more than $25 are passed off as expensive art. With today's state-of-the-art equipment, it's easy to produce thousands of fraudulent but impressive copies, all marked with phony edition numbers and forged signatures.

In past years, works by Dalí, Miró, Picasso, and Chagall have been subject to counterfeiting, and when large networks have been uncovered through sting operations, even legitimate works by the artists have suffered a price drop.

Because art fraud is a widespread and highly sophisticated business, detecting worthless duplications involves more than applying common-sense guidelines. If you contemplate investing in expensive art, you'd do well to commit to serious study before becoming a buyer. It's wise to take classes, read books, and deal only with reputable galleries and auction houses.

Limited Editions That Aren't

One other art scam involves limited editions. One unknowing couple purchased a lithograph numbered 12/500, signifying that the work was twelfth off the press in a series of five hundred and therefore of special value.

But several years later, when they wanted to sell the piece, an appraiser informed the pair that instead of merely five hundred prints in circulation, there were literally thousands! Taken aback by their naïveté, the couple did some investigating and discovered that the number 500 referred only to the number of prints in "Series A." Unfortunately for these and other investors, there was also a "Series B," "Series C," and so on, until the total was well into five figures.

If you decide to purchase a limited-edition lithograph or serigraph, be sure you buy from a knowledgeable dealer who certifies, in writing, the total number of published prints.

Pyramid Schemes

Pyramid schemes have been around for a long time and seem to have great survival instincts. They adapt and mutate like viruses and continue to pop up in various incarnations. No sooner does one pyramid operation make headlines than a new ("perfectly legal") program starts circulating.

All strata of society are targeted by pyramids, from the privileged to down-and-outers seeking to make the quick buck. Although they are outlawed in most states, various ruses are used to skirt the legalities. Perhaps the reason this kind of scam continues to thrive is that it appeals to our most noble as well as self-serving instincts. Pyramids generally rely on well-intentioned individuals who, in good faith, recruit their friends. They appeal to our desire to share a "once-in-a-lifetime opportunity" with others while benefiting ourselves. And often pitch letters include the phrase "This is NOT a pyramid scheme!"

One operation requires that participants "invest" $1,500, for example, and to make it easy, credit cards are accepted. In theory the program makes sense. When eight friends pay out $1,500, the person at the top of the list receives $12,000. And in turn, so does everyone else. But like all pyramids, the hypothesis works only as long as the machine is fed a constant stream of new players. When new investors run thin, those at the bottom of the list are out of money and out of luck.

It's difficult to trace where these schemes actually originate, for once set in motion, they spread like wildfire, taking on regional characteristics and buzzwords as they move from state to state. In trendy California they might be tailored to appeal to New Agers, while in the Bible Belt they often adopt religious overtones.

When a pyramid game comes to the attention of law enforcement, winners are sometimes contacted and urged to return their windfall to those below them on the ladder. In other instances, winners are subject to prosecution. When given the opportunity to make things right, most people are willing to cooperate and refund money to those who got stung. But a few hard-core enthusiasts maintain that pyramid games create victims only when they are forced to stop.

The problem is that nothing lasts forever, and where there are winners, there will ultimately be losers. So the next time a friend sends you a "completely legal" chain letter (also a form of pyramid scheme), or an invitation to join a pyramid game, remember that sooner or later someone is going to turn up empty-handed. And unless you start out near the top of the heap, that someone could easily be you.

WHO'S WHO ANTHOLOGIES: THE HIGH COST OF VANITY

Those who might not otherwise dream of investing in anything less secure than blue chips might still fall prey to investments in vanity. Mrs. Jones, as I'll call her, was a character right out of a novel. She came to the United States as a teenage immigrant, speaking virtually no English. Working two jobs to help her family, she learned a new language and put herself through college. In time she worked her way up the corporate ladder in the same company where her mother once scrubbed floors.

Convinced that the American dream could be achieved, this plucky woman began to enjoy her hard-earned rewards. She married and became a homeowner and proudly displayed the awards she'd won throughout the years in various community organizations. One day she received a letter on quality stock with an embossed letterhead, asking for information about her accomplishments that could be included in a national publication. Mrs. Jones was thrilled.

The book, she learned, would feature successful women like herself, outstanding achievers in business and the community. The price of the limited edition was several hundred dollars, but it seemed a small enough price for such an honor.

A scam? Rip-off? Much like the poetry contests that publish participants' poems for a hefty price, this is a legitimate operation as long as the company follows through with its claims. The question is one of values. The ego is targeted here, and for some, seeing their name in an impressive volume is worth every penny. But if you are thinking of shelling out beaucoup bucks for a dubious claim to fame, you might want to reconsider. The bona fide "Who's Who" books are in the library and shouldn't be confused with vanity press imitators. If vanity is the issue, there are less expensive ways to grab some glory.

TRADE SCHOOL RIP-OFFS

Certainly the best investment a young person can make is in education. To some this means a four-year college and perhaps graduate work. But to millions of others whose skills are primarily nonacademic, trade schools seem to offer the surest road to success.

A young high school dropout thought his life was taking a turn for the better when he encountered a recruiter from a trade institute who offered him $5 to sign up for courses. He signed on the dotted line, got his money, and began to think he might have a future. A few weeks later he received a letter informing him that his future was, in fact, in hock. He owed several thousand dollars on a "student loan" even though he had yet to attend a single class.

In another instance a young ex-convict was placed in a trade school course for executive secretaries. Needless to say, basic reading was not part of the school's curriculum. When a private group that helps parolees establish themselves in mainstream society rated her reading skills, the woman tested at the first-grade level. In still another case, a student was promised that if she couldn't repay her government-backed loan, the school would assume her debt, and the recruiter assured her that as soon as she enrolled they would find her lucrative part-time work. Both pledges proved worthless, and the student found herself hard-pressed to repay her loan.

In each of these instances, the young and needy were promised a foot up on the success ladder only to find themselves worse off than before. It's been estimated that as many as two million students sign up at learning institutions whose empty promises force taxpayers to pick up the tab for nearly a billion dollars in uncollectable student loans.

There are, of course, many trade schools that deliver an invaluable education to their students. But the dream busters who don't deliver hurt all levels of society, from scammed students who might lose heart and never try again to overburdened taxpayers. Some of these schools are outright fraudulent, while others are simply not as good as their advertising copy. Schools in the latter category may employ inferior teachers and fail to give students the instruction they really need to compete.

Anyone enrolling in a trade, business, or beauty college should do some homework before signing any papers. The easiest way to research a particular school is to check on accreditation and ask for the names of several former students.

"*A*FFINITY" *S*CAMS—*B*ETRAYAL FROM *W*ITHIN

The matriarch of an immigrant family took great pride in her frugality, her ability to prosper in a foreign country, and most of all, in her children. Her son had just been admitted to a prominent university, and her daughter was about to graduate from medical school.

When an American friend talked about women's liberation and suggested that she might benefit from coming to one of their support groups, this mother and business owner just smiled. She was her family's CEO and made all the decisions regarding investments. She had placed some of the profits from her family's business in money market accounts, but she also invested in blue-chip stocks and mutual funds that specialized in convertible bonds.

"Strictly triple-A rated," she used to say. "We want to keep our money secure." But one evening a friend of her second cousin stopped by for tea and told her about an investment fund that had recently been created exclusively by and for those in from her country. "Just our people," he explained. "Everyone's getting into it."

Although she normally wouldn't have touched anything remotely speculative, the woman welcomed a chance to invest her family's money in a way that would show solidarity with her friends and neighbors. In the spirit of community, she handed the friend-of-a-cousin a large check.

When monthly statements were not forthcoming, she first listened to excuses, then, when the friend's number was disconnected, she began to make whispered inquiries. The investment expert, it seems, hadn't been seen or heard from for more than a month.

It wasn't long before this normally shrewd and discerning woman realized her error. Thousands of her family's hard-earned dollars had been lost because she had trusted one of her own. Embarrassment and "loss of face" prevented her from contacting the police, which is exactly what the scammer had counted on.

There have been a growing number of confidence schemes, called "affinity scams," perpetrated by those who prey on people with similar associations. Sometimes they operate outside the law, absconding with the funds entrusted to them, and other times they simply pressure friends into investment programs that are inferior to those of mainstream institutions. In all cases they exploit the natural bonds that unify and obligate members of insular groups. The association is often ethnic, but it can also be based on religion, a twelve-step recovery group, or even a business-oriented club. Members of any tight-knit group who are approached by one of their own should evaluate what is offered by their usual prudent standards. Betrayal from within is as seductive as it is cruel.

Life Insurance Agents Who Churn Accounts

Most people who have dabbled even briefly in the stock market know enough to avoid brokers who churn accounts. Rather than encouraging clients to invest for the long term, these hustlers encourage them to buy and sell frequently, thus generating more commissions.

While this type of wheeling-dealing is a common practice in the securities business, most people don't realize that a similar type of hustle can occur when they purchase life insurance. There has been a recent surge among agents who pad their income by advising insurance clients to change or add to their existing policies. They offer reduced rates for special or additional coverage, often touting the benefits of a policy switch. What they don't always tell you is that you may have to pay significant surrender fees when changing policies, or that new payments, however low, may be deducted from a policy's cash value.

If your insurance agent suggests any change in your existing policy, it's wise to get a second or third (unbiased) opinion before making any new commitments. It's the best insurance against churning specialists.

Never Write a Check to the IRS

A young West Coast couple finally did it. After years of pulling all-nighters on April 14, then standing in long post office lines to make sure they mailed in their tax return under the wire, the Smiths were finally ahead of schedule. They had their forms filled out, signed, and enclosed with a check by the end of March. Pleased with themselves for beating that old demon procrastination, they celebrated with a well-earned dinner at their favorite bistro.

You can imagine their distress when several months later they received a notice that they owned Uncle Sam $900 plus interest and penalties.

"But we paid!" screamed the wife.

"We got back a canceled check!" exclaimed the husband. "Didn't we?"

After a few moments of hand-wringing, the couple sorted through their records and found their canceled checks from the month of April. Sure enough, there was a check in the amount of $900, exactly the amount they owed—and had paid—the IRS. But on closer inspection the couple found that their $900 check had indeed been cashed—by a Mrs. Jones!

Instead of making out the check to the Internal Revenue Service, the wife had used the familiar (and quite legal) abbreviation IRS. The trouble is that at some point their check ended up in the wrong hands, and the thief changed the capital *I* to an *M*, causing the initials to read not IRS but MRS. Then the last name Jones was carefully added.

Don't let your enthusiasm to pay Uncle Sam make you vulnerable to this scam. Take an extra few seconds and write out the complete name. You might not like paying taxes, but you'll like it even less if you end up paying a private party!

Mutual Funds That Aren't What They Seem

Mutual funds are thought by many to be the safest way to invest in the stock market. Unlike buying a single stock (tantamount to placing all one's eggs in a single basket), mutual funds offer investors a way to hedge their bets while availing themselves of growth and income opportunities.

The problem is that what you see isn't always what you get. When the stock market is bullish, almost anyone can make money, but when faced with the challenge of hard times, it's not unusual for mutual fund managers to go out on a limb. Although it's not illegal for managers to change existing strategies, investors' dollars may not always be distributed as promised.

For example, a fund that is described as investing in insured bonds may in fact have a percentage of its portfolio in bonds that are uninsured. This shift may result in higher returns, or it may produce higher losses.

Funds that call themselves growth and income funds may provide income only in the technical sense. They might yield no more than a fraction of a percentage point of annual income, far less than any bank or money market account.

Before investing in a mutual fund, study its performance over the past decade. Then carefully read the prospectus. It's against SEC regulations for a mutual fund to handle investors' money in a manner not specified in the prospectus. But sometimes, subtly hidden among pages and pages of text, they may state that in certain situations the fund manager has the leeway to change course. The trouble is, the average person usually lacks the expertise really to understand these complex documents. If you plan to invest seriously, it is wise either to take a course on how to read a prospectus or hire an expert to check over the fine print.

Customers Who Buy and Run

When most people hear the term "bust-out" they think of a jailbreak. But to those in the know, a bust-out is a scam, one that has become prevalent in recent years.

After nearly two decades of working for other people, a California couple decided to cash in their savings and start a small restaurant supply business. They used their garage as an office and a rented a nearby warehouse. It wasn't easy, but they were thrilled finally to be their own bosses.

Because their state was recovering slowly from the recession, many credit ratings, both individual and corporate, had been affected. Willing to give others a chance, the new business owners allowed their customers considerable leeway when it came to financial arrangements. It wasn't unusual for them to deliver merchandise and wait sixty to ninety days for payment.

Most of their orders were small ones, but they built up a steady clientele and were beginning to show consistent profits. One day a man called from San Diego, requesting a few hundred dollars' worth of supplies. The couple was impressed that one of his references was a top national corporation, and they did only a perfunctory credit check.

A shipment was sent to the new client, and the invoice was paid within thirty days. The next month the customer reordered and again took care of his bill in record time. Then he wrote a letter explaining that he was expanding his operation and placed an order for more than $30,000 of merchandise. Because he was already an established customer, and one who had credit with a major firm, the couple shipped off their wares and waited for a check.

Unfortunately, it never arrived. When thirty, then sixty days passed, the couple sent follow-up invoices and finally a past-due notice. When ninety days came and went with no new order and no payment, they called their customer. His number was disconnected.

What these business owners experienced was not unusual. These scam artists order merchandise on credit from small businesses, often mom-and-pop operations, then resell the stock and pocket their gains. They frequently carry out a tiny transaction with a major company to establish a credible track record and an impressive reference. And sometimes they pay a couple of small bills with the firm they intend to sting, to pave the way for the big one. Once they have the large quantity of goods in their possession, they make themselves scarce, and the business owners are left empty-handed and out of luck.

Company owners should be diligent about checking the credit references of all new customers and do extra research when an existing client places an unusually large order. If there is any question about reliability, you might even visit the customer's business address to make sure it's not just a post office box with Voicemail. There are also business trade groups you can join, whose members are allowed access to credit data. If you have already let the horse out of the barn, you can contact the fraud division of the local police department. Better yet, contact them before doing business with anyone who seems suspect.

CREDIT CARD RATE WARS

Credit card companies are falling all over themselves these days to steal your business away from their competitors. Anyone with a decent credit history is likely to get an offer or two a week from outfits that advertise no annual fee and a low interest rate. They inform you that you can use the preapproved enclosed form to transfer your balance from other cards.

So what's there to lose? There's certainly nothing wrong with taking advantage of price or rate wars, but read the fine print. Those low-low-interest credit card rates are good for only a limited time. After the (usually brief) introductory period they revert back to their prevailing rate, which could be even higher than what you're currently paying.

As long as it's a buyer's market, you might want to consider taking advantage of such offers. But do read the fine print with an eye toward the long term. And remember that lowering your interest rate doesn't reduce your debt, and it may even give you an excuse to increase it.

10

REAL ESTATE RIP-OFFS

Aside from investing in oneself, real estate, particularly home ownership, is the most basic, enduring, and rewarding investment one can make. Although recent recession years have seen property values take a plunge, the long-term picture is still bright. Owning one's home is the best way to stay abreast of inflation while enjoying the investment dollar on a daily basis.

Rental properties, second trust deeds, and real estate stocks can often provide extra income, but they are encumbered with more risk than a primary residence. As in any milieu where money changes hands, scam artists stand ready to take advantage of the unsuspecting. Those who specialize in real property and its financing are prolific and not always easy to detect.

Tenants from Hell

An engineer who dabbled in real estate invested some of his earnings in an upscale residence in a desirable part of town. He purchased the three-bedroom home for a good price, then added a hot tub, landscaping, and an extra bath. A real estate agent provided him with a list of prospective tenants.

Finally he selected a nice family with two children and requested the usual "first and last," along with a security deposit. All went well until the next payment was due. When no check arrived in the mail, the landlord called his renter.

"Oh, we're just a little behind. We'll get a check off by the end of the week."

Not in this lifetime. No payment arrived that week or the next. Now the "last" month's payment had to be used for the second month. Hoping against hope that his renters had merely hit a snag in their cash flow, the owner called and asked how he could help them work things out. His reward for trying to be a nice guy was one more empty promise.

Frantic, and with no real experience to draw on, he called his attorney. Two days later he received the bad news: His renters, it seems, had filed for bankruptcy and the bottom line wasn't pretty. Even if they failed to pay one more penny (which at this point seemed likely), they couldn't be evicted until the bankruptcy had been resolved.

Meanwhile, the owner was obligated to continue making monthly mortgage payments, and hefty ones at that. In addition to the lost rental income, he now had legal fees and court costs. Overall he would be out over $20,000 by the time the deadbeats finally vacated the premises.

To add insult to injury, the owner did some investigating and found that this wasn't the renters' first bankruptcy. More significantly, it wasn't the first time they had failed to meet their obligations. Leasing expensive homes and then ducking payments was apparently a way of life for these experienced scam artists, who always managed to operate just within the fringes of the law!

At least this landlord availed himself of good counsel. When the eviction at long last became final, he had learned enough to change the locks on the house immediately. For if a tenant re-enters the premises the day of eviction, and thus reclaims possession, the process must start all over again.

Keep in mind that real estate agents may not check the references of prospective tenants thoroughly enough, and some don't bother at all. This is a case where that old ounce of prevention is worth its weight in gold. A smart landlord will run his or her own credit check on prospective tenants before they sign a lease.

Loan Brokers Who Run Deceptive Ads

With the recent recession taking a huge toll on real estate prices, particularly in states like California, many valuable properties have been reclaimed by the banks. When these homes are resold as "bank repos," they can create lucrative buying opportunities for amateurs and professionals alike.

One hopeful home buyer in Sacramento was browsing through the classifieds and saw an ad that sparked his interest: a three-bedroom, two-bath house in a desirable location. He called the number listed and was greeted by a man's voice. Before he had a chance make any inquiries, he was bluntly asked, "Are you prequalified for a loan?" When he answered affirmatively, the line went dead.

Perplexed, he called back and asked a few probing questions of his own. What he learned was that the advertised house didn't exist. It was simply a come-on, a trick used by a mortgage broker to reel in customers. While the man who ran the ad may have been conducting a legitimate loan business, his method of attracting clients was certainly less than straightforward. Which makes one suspect his ethics in general.

If you encounter loan brokers through such a ruse, think twice before doing business with them. A recommendation from a trusted banker or attorney is less likely to provoke remorse.

Time-Shares Can Cost More than They Are Worth

A woman driving across the country some years ago stopped to visit a friend in Telluride, Colorado, the elegant ski resort where Donald Trump later celebrated his second marriage. At that time, however, the town wasn't as well known, and the woman figured that prices were on the way up. How right she was. She purchased a small condo on which monthly payments are made by a steady stream of renters, and within a year the value of her property doubled.

Most people, however, who invest in vacation property or time-shares don't do as well. Those who want the comfort and convenience of a condominium often choose to buy into a time-share, thinking they'll save money on hotel and restaurant bills. But a $15,000 time-share can jump to over $25,000 in the course of several years, as management and maintenance fees hike up the costs. And if you use the place one week every year for seven years, your cost will average out to over $500 a night! For that price one could stay in a luxury suite at a world-class resort.

Unless you plan to spend a great deal of time at a vacation home, you're probably better off spending your money on commercial lodgings. In any event, check with your accountant before making a purchase and let him or her determine whether the numbers make good sense.

Bank Errors That Cost You Thousands

In recent years throughout the nation, and especially in places like California, lower interest rates have enabled many homeowners to refinance their mortgages and reduce their monthly payments.

Most of us make our mortgage payments routinely, if not electronically, and we assume that those payments are in order. Recently, a Southern California resident was unable to make several payments on his six-figure adjustable-rate mortgage. Understandably worried that he might be flirting with foreclosure, he thought about consulting an attorney. But in preparing information to give to his lawyer, he hit pay dirt. Instead of being in arrears, he discovered that the bank owed *him* more than

$30,000. In a separate incident, another borrower found that, had he not done his homework, over the life of his loan he would have overpaid his friendly lenders a cool million dollars!

Whoa, how does something like that happen? Banks don't make mistakes. Or do they? According to a recent General Accounting Office study, these situations were hardly glaring exceptions to the rule. On the contrary, they found that up to 25 percent of all adjustable-rate mortgages (ARMs) may contain errors.

In the wake of these findings, banks have been put on notice by the comptroller of the currency that they may be subject to liability. While it's thought that most of these errors are relatively small and occur because of the complicated nature of ARMs, it's estimated that net overcharges may total at least $10 billion. Any one or a combination of errors can throw the numbers off track and keep them there as discrepancies accrue. In most cases these blunders are unintentional. But that doesn't lessen the damage to the borrower, and bankers are not thrilled to admit to miscalculations. Chances are slim that they're going to come knocking on your door, refund check in hand.

If you have an adjustable-rate mortgage, you may want to do some checking of your own. For a small fee ($40 or so) you can hire an ARM auditor to review your loan documents. If mistakes are found, he or she can advise you on how to obtain reimbursement.

11

T HE

B EAUTY

G AME

A popular television newsmagazine recently ran an segment that showed several pairs of actors in various situations. One person on each team was remarkably good-looking and the other was, well, ordinary. The twosomes were filmed with hidden cameras while applying for jobs and seeking help when a car had run out of gas. Each paired actor or actress was dressed alike and given almost identical résumés.

In literally every case, the more attractive person was offered the job, even when the "ordinary" person was told he or she had outstanding qualifications. And while the plainer young woman, who was clearly in distress, merely received directions to the nearest gas station, the stranded "looker" had several men go out of their way to bring her containers filled with gasoline.

Such discrimination is hardly fair, but it is a universal fact of life. Beauty (or the lack of it), however superficial, does influence the way people relate to us and consequently heavily affects every aspect of our lives. It's no wonder, then, that men and women alike are susceptible to products and services that promise to enhance our looks. And in this age of rapidly expanding technology, new discoveries, from thigh creams to laser lifts, are crowding into an already overloaded marketplace.

$\mathscr{A}$NTIWRINKLE $\mathscr{L}$OTIONS

Magazines and television continually invade our consciousness with trigger words such as "rejuvenate," "revolutionary," "European formula," and "laboratory results." Interpreting "adspeak" is a monumental task in a highly competitive field where beauty and grooming manufacturers often make claims just this side of scandalous. While they might not come out and say that their cream or lotion will make you look ten years younger, they do promise fresher, clearer, or younger-looking skin. Which prompts us to ask: Fresher than what? Younger than whom?

Often the copy on cosmetic advertisements seems to be stolen right from the pages of romance novels. Adjectives such as "seductive," "indulgent," and "shameless" are used to describe hair coloring and skin cream, perhaps in the hope that if the consumer's appearance isn't noticeably changed, at least she will feel pampered and perhaps a bit daring.

More than one manufacturer claims to combine science and nature, the best of both worlds. But how can any such product be otherwise? Any potion made from plants or animals, or their by-products, is of course, natural. And anything that is combined with other ingredients in a container is certainly a product of "science."

We rely, of course, on advertising to keep us apprised of sales, new products, and improvements in existing merchandise. Ads are a valuable aid to shoppers, and there's no question that the good ones add to the quality of our lives. And we're not naive. We all know that wearing a certain fragrance won't change a wallflower into a femme fatale, but dazzling ads are calculated to play on our subconscious, our emotions, our hopes, and our fantasies.

So assuming we know that a great deal of advertising copy is pure hype, but we still wish to avail ourselves of the best products, how do we make an intelligent choice? While most commercial lotions smooth and protect the skin, they generally don't do much actually to diminish wrinkles. Even creams that contain the acclaimed alpha hydroxy acids usually aren't strong enough significantly to alter the skin. And the term "laboratory tested" usually means tested for safety not efficacy.

If you are seriously interested in improving your skin, you should consult a dermatologist, who may, if appropriate, prescribe a cream or lotion that contains higher percentages of ingredients that cause the skin to peel and regenerate, and has been FDA tested for effectiveness. But even the strongest medication on the market won't perform miracles.

What Plastic Surgeons Don't Want You to Know

No one wants to undergo surgery if it's avoidable. Still, millions of men and women submit to the plastic surgeon's scalpel every year, and the number is increasing rapidly. Actors and others in the limelight make up just a fraction of cosmetic surgery patients. As the youth-conscious baby boom generation begins to gray, and with the competitive job market giving the nod to youthful executives, the beauty business is thriving.

And the growing demand is being matched by new and better technologies. Face-lifts that merely stretched the skin, resulting in a masklike appearance, have been replaced by techniques that tighten underlying muscles to provide a more natural look. And broken veins, birthmarks, wrinkles, and other skin blemishes can now be eliminated with state-of-the-art lasers. Bags under the eyes can be removed without incisions, saddlebags can be suctioned from flabby thighs, and fat can be borrowed from areas where you don't want it (like your stomach) and added to breasts, cheeks, and aging hands. With all these advances, there's an abundance of procedures for the beauty-motivated to choose from. But with high-tech advancements come the need for greater consumer knowledge.

There was a time when no reputable doctor advertised his or her services. But the promotion of physicians, hospitals, and specific procedures, especially in the highly competitive field of cosmetic surgery, is now considered legitimate.

onsumers need to be aware of are misleading ads. Often plas-
s advertise a particular operation, with before-and-after photographs accompanying the text. It's wise to keep in mind the fact that
successful plastic surgery usually results in subtle rather than dramatic
improvements. If an "after" photo looks remarkably better than the "before" picture, study it carefully. Some surgeons display photographs of
patients who have indeed undergone a particular procedure, along with
several others! If a lower eye-lift has turned a plain guy into a prince, scru-
tinize his face for other alterations. Have his nose and chin been subtly
sculpted? Have his upper lids been tightened as well?

In pictures of women, be sure to compare hairstyle and makeup. And
in all cases, consider lighting. Bad or good lighting can add or subtract
more years from a person's face than any surgery. A woman who has undergone blepharoplasty (eye-lift) may look twenty years younger if, in her
"after" photo, she has the advantage of professional makeup, hairstyling,
and lighting.

The key here is to have realistic expectations, based on valid appraisals.
A good doctor will tell you approximately how many years might be
rolled back with a face- or eye-lift. And most plastic surgery offices now
offer computer imaging so you can see what changes a procedure will
make on your unique features.

It's also wise to make sure you're up-to-date on the latest techniques.
For example, until recently, a complete face-lift was the only option for
men and women in search of a firmer jawline. But today, patients and
doctors can assess the problem and consider a number of procedures, including facial liposuction to remove excess fat from below the chin, and
endoscopic surgery, where only small incisions are made to allow the surgeon access to the droopy area. Frown and forehead lines can be resolved
with a corona lift, fat or collagen injections, or dermabrasion or laser
peels. There are even some dermatologists and plastic surgeons who, in
the course of an office visit, can inject you with a neurotoxin that inhibits
your ability to frown, causing old lines to be diminished and new ones
prevented.

Sometimes the least expensive and least invasive procedure is the best.
Other times there is a valid reason to choose the most complex and expensive solution. The point is to be as knowledgeable as possible before

consulting a surgeon, so that you're well aware of all the options and can ask discerning questions.

When selecting a surgeon, even for an initial consultation, most people know enough to choose a doctor who is "board certified." But that term can be misleading. The only board recognized by the American Board of Specialties is the American Board of Plastic Surgery. Members must be qualified by an examination and strict educational requirements. Once a member of this board, physicians may choose to join the American Society of Plastic and Reconstructive Surgeons (ASPRS).

For referrals or information on a specific physician or procedure, call the ASPRS toll-free at (800) 635-0635. The number for the American Board of Plastic Surgery is (215) 587-9322.

"Cures" for Baldness

While women agonize over the fat on their thighs, men most often complain about hair loss. A great deal of excitement was generated a few years ago when doctors discovered that a blood pressure medication called minoxidil sometimes stimulated hair growth. Men began flocking to their physicians' offices, hoping to walk out looking like Fabio.

Was it just hype? The answer here is a qualified no and a big however. Yes, there is evidence that minoxidil restores *some* growth in *some* individuals. But more often than not, the new hair more closely resembles peach fuzz than Samson-like locks, and for some reason not everyone gains even that result.

If you're a fellow who's concerned over a receding hairline, or a woman who has experienced hair loss, you might ask your doctor for a prescription for minoxidil and see what does or doesn't sprout. If that fails to revive hair growth, the other options are toupees, hair weaves or extensions, and hair transplants. For the latter you will need to consult with a plastic surgeon who specializes in hair grafts and scalp reductions.

What you shouldn't do is spend hope and money on any over-the-counter creams or balms that even hint at restoring your hair. If there were a product out there that really produced results, it would be headline news and the company's stock would soar through the roof.

$\mathcal{S}$CAM $\mathcal{A}$RTISTS $\mathcal{W}$HO $\mathcal{P}$REY ON $\mathcal{T}$EENS

Kate was an attractive fifteen-year-old, with blond hair, a clear complexion, and a slim figure. But teenagers are, by definition, dissatisfied with their appearance. The emergence of a pimple on prom night is not a dermatological occurrence, it's a disaster. And a body that carries either too many or too few pounds can encourage ridicule. Just as the older population has special vulnerabilities, those struggling through the agonies of adolescence are prime targets for scam artists hawking so-called beauty aids.

Because Kate didn't consider herself as well endowed as some of her peers, she was ripe for a product advertised in a teen magazine, offering amazing results. She used her allowance to cover the cost of a jar of hormone cream that would supposedly increase her breast size in record time. The good news is that the cream was probably as harmless as it was ineffective. Estrogen is a prescription drug, and any over-the-counter product claiming to contain it will have only an inconsequential amount. Yet ads for these creams and lotions often show "before" and "after" pictures, with a grim-faced, flat-chested young woman appearing next to a smiling damsel with voluptuous breasts.

For several weeks Kate meticulously applied the contents of the jar (mailed to her in a plain brown wrapper), and every day she checked her mirror for results. At one point she thought she was actually seeing some progress. But then she realized that she had gained five pounds and had added a bit of cushion on her hips as well.

Realizing that her experiment had failed, she now studied ads selling exercise contraptions that guaranteed to add inches to one's chest. While it's true that the muscles behind the breasts can be developed through workouts, the breasts themselves will not be affected. Still, hope springs eternal. Kate, who felt she'd rather die than discuss her perceived inadequacies, sent off a money order for a bust "enhancer."

Again she lost money and failed to gain the promised inches. However, over the next year her breasts grew (as her mother kept telling her they would), and she's no longer self-conscious.

Girls faced with pressure to resemble the model-of-the-month are concerned with every extra pound. A recent survey suggested that Caucasian girls (as opposed to African Americans, who have a more positive body image) consider the perfect figure to be about 5'6" or 5'7" and around 110 pounds. Model-size, to be sure, but hardly a configuration that normal women of any age can easily attain. Yet pressure to fulfill the fantasy is so great that some girls begin dieting in grade school.

Diet pills, diuretics, and even laxatives are targeted at the teen and even preteen market. Most of them are worthless, and some are outright dangerous. Certainly anything that contributes to a binge-and-purge eating disorder is a serious health threat. And so-called diet pills that contain phyenylpropanolamine can elevate blood pressure, contribute to anxiety and insomnia, and become addictive.

While young girls are easy marks for products that promise to remove pounds or add curves, boys are the targets for steroid and "muscle building" formulas. High schoolers who want to excel at sports and impress the girls are quick to spend money on worthless and sometimes dangerous products. While the human growth hormone (HGH) is sometimes used to promote growth in children who are diagnosed with medical problems, its use for aesthetic purposes is not FDA approved and can produce serious side effects. Unfortunately, there is a black market for all drugs, including HGH and anabolic steroids.

Of less serious concern, but in the rip-off category, are phony steroids and "athlete's drinks" that claim to help build a brawny physique. Products in this group usually contain nothing more than vitamins, minerals, and ingredients such as algae or wheat grass. While all of these items have nutritional value, they can best be acquired through a good diet or generic (and far less expensive) supplements.

Parents should be aware of their teens' sense of image and self-esteem. Kids who are encouraged to talk about themselves, their feelings, and how they think they look are less likely to fall prey to worthless and sometimes destructive products.

THIGH CREAMS

If there is one part of a woman's body that seems to cause perpetual torment, it's her thighs. The vast majority of women consider theirs to be too large, and even those with otherwise svelte figures frequently complain of that dreaded dimpling called cellulite.

There have always been thigh creams on the market, promising to restore smoothness to rippling "saddlebags." In the past, these products were generally found on the back shelves along with potions that claim to grow hair and increase breast size. And who knows? In some cases their ingredients may have been interchangeable.

But in the 1990s, thigh creams are serious business. Top cosmetic companies now offer full lines of cellulite-reducing products; trendy spas offer treatments that include body wraps, special massages, and electronic zapping; and newspapers and magazines run ads touting the latest thigh-reducing concoctions.

Has science really stumbled onto a cure for this universal blight? Or has the snake oil merely been repackaged? While those affiliated with cosmetic firms may insist that the war has been won, many experts disagree. Cellulite, which is nothing more than pockets of fat that love to nest in thigh tissue, can perhaps be broken up a bit by a combination of balms and battering. In some instances, as with a facial, the skin may take on a smoother, glowing appearance for several hours after treatment.

But in the long run, diet and exercise are the only natural ways to improve one's figure in general, and thighs in particular. It's helpful to remember that most women are born with a genetic predisposition toward fleshy flanks. (The cavewomen who preceded us simply didn't make it through the winter unless they had the kind of body that efficiently stored fat.) For those stubborn pockets of flesh that won't respond to either diet or discipline, new techniques in liposuction performed by a good plastic surgeon may provide the solution.

12

$\mathcal{S}$HOW $\mathcal{B}$USINESS $\mathcal{S}$CAMS

In Southern California, where the air is thick with celluloid dreams, the movie industry lures daily busloads of wannabes from around the country. New York, also a hub for modeling, television, and theater, attracts more than its fair share of those seeking fame and fortune. In both these arenas, there exists a subindustry of borderline scammers who prey, quite successfully, on the young and the hopeful.

FORREST $\mathcal{G}$UMP IN THE RED: *$#@! HAPPENS!

In Hollywood, everybody wants a piece of the action. A writer, actor, or director is considered fortunate if he or she can finagle a percentage of a film's profits. Winston Groom, author of the novel *Forrest Gump*, and Eric Roth, screenwriter of the blockbuster film, seemed set for life when they were promised a small slice of *Gump*'s net revenues. So why have these trusting souls been told that at the end of 1994 there were no earnings to share? It seems they weren't the ones who got to define the term "net."

With $661 million in box office receipts, and licensing fees for *Gump*-inspired paraphernalia expected to bring in another $350 million, it seems safe to say that *Gump* has been a resounding success. But according to Hollywood bean counters, the film lost $62 million. Come again? Were the accountants the most creative members of the team? Here's what they say:

After collecting its $191 million share of box office receipts, Paramount took its distribution fee off the top (32 percent of the gross). This hefty amount does not include advertising and distribution costs, which are tallied up in another category. Most of this distribution fee, over $61 million, is pure profit.

And that's before the "overhead" fee, which is 10 percent of the distribution expenses. Add $6.7 million. So far, total distribution costs approach $135 million, before we even figure in the $112 million to produce the film. Are you still with me? Studio "overhead" is another $14.5 million, plus $6 million for interest on the negative costs. And so forth. All told, Paramount came up $62 million in the red.

The venerable humorist Art Buchwald suffered a fate similar to that of Groom and Roth when Paramount claimed that the 1988 Eddie Murphy hit *Coming to America* was also a loser. Buchwald and his partner won over $1 million in a legal battle.

So what's a poor writer (or actor) to do? Those in the know suggest demanding a piece of the gross, as opposed to the net profit, or else insisting on a fat fee up front. The "back end," as percentage points are sometimes called, often ends up being more of a fantasy than anything on the screen.

$\mathcal{A}$CTORS' "$\mathcal{A}$GENTS"

The list is long. It includes every girl who was ever (almost) a prom queen, every mother's beautiful child, and every young man who can tear up a room with his guitar. They kiss their moms and sweethearts good-bye, climb on a Greyhound, and peer out the back window as Small-Town America becomes a speck in the distance. Finally, they arrive in Tinseltown, where the only stars they see are made of brass, shining up from the sidewalk. But, hey, this is Hollywood, and they're going to take it by storm.

The first thing our girl from Omaha does is land a job waiting tables in a little coffee shop on Sunset Boulevard. She hopes she'll be discovered there, but most of her customers are tourists or folks who look a little strange. But she works hard, joins an acting class, and religiously reads *Variety* and *The Hollywood Reporter*. She gets brave and goes on a "cattle call" for a small role in a TV pilot. Her credits include the role of Maggie in *Cat on a Hot Tin Roof*, but high school plays don't seem to have much cachet in La La Land.

The small-town girl hears the old conundrum: You can't get a job without an agent, and you can't get an agent without a job. She calls some of the better-known talent agencies and is politely instructed to send in her pictures and bio. She carefully mails off her yearbook picture and a list of high school credits, and never hears a word.

One day, as she's walking down the boulevard, a middle-aged man in sunglasses inquires if she's ever done any modeling. Well, just in her mom's tennis club fashion show. To her surprise, the man gives her his card and tells her to call. Several of his models, he tells her, have gone on to get parts in feature films.

A warning bell sounds, but our young lady can't afford not to check it out. She makes an appointment and shows up the next day at a seedy-looking office in North Hollywood. She looks around at stacks of magazines with pictures of naked girls draped in whips, chains, and other paraphernalia she can't even name. She may be young and naïve, but she's heard of the old casting couch routine. She's outta there.

That night at the restaurant, she pours coffee for one of her last customers. He asks if she's an actress, and she wryly answers that she's trying to be. The fellow's fairly young, well, not too much over thirty, and he seems nice. He knows how hard it is, he says, and inquires about her experience. Still a bit shaken by her trek to that awful girlie magazine, she tells him of her narrow escape.

The guy laughs with her and then casually mentions that he's an agent. Our young lady's heart stops. A real agent. He probably handles only big stars. But maybe he can give her a little advice. How does somebody ever get her first break?

Well, the agent says, "I sometimes take on new clients. You know, they're always looking for new faces, especially on TV. Do you have your photos?"

The aspiring actress tells him she has a black-and-white glossy of her senior picture, and he tells her to bring it with her and stop by his office tomorrow. Wow. He doesn't have to ask twice.

At one o'clock sharp, Miss Hopeful arrives at the agent's modest but decent office. No naked ladies here. She shows him her photo. "You photograph nicely," he says. "When you get your portfolio together I think we can start by getting you some auditions for commercials. At least that way you'll get some exposure and a little bit of money. And that's how you build a résumé."

She's in heaven. She's on her way. The agent tells her that producers will need to see a photo composite: several close-ups, one nice bathing suit shot, and a couple in casual clothes and business attire. Oh, dear. She doesn't own a business suit, and, uh, how much will the photos cost?

Not to worry. The agent knows a talented young photographer who works with aspiring actors. What is she, a size six? He's got a wardrobe she can choose from, good designer stuff, and he'll do her pictures for about half of what it would cost her elsewhere. What a guy.

Even so, the photo session isn't cheap; it sets our waitress back a few hundred. But after all, it's the cost of doing business, and that's what savings are for. The shoot itself is fun and the photographer is awfully nice. A week later the budding actress receives her pictures and is pleased with how good she looks. Who said Hollywood is a tough town?

She calls her agent, tells him she has her pictures, and asks if he would like her to sign anything. Hmmm? Oh, sure. He's pretty busy for the next few days, but can she come around next week?

Our girl worries because the agent didn't seem so "busy" before. But a week later she drops off her photos at his office and signs her name on an agent's agreement. Now she's official. All she has to do is wait for that all-important first job.

And so she waits. And waits. And waits on tables. When she calls her agent she gets his secretary or a machine saying, "Sorry, we're out of the office right now, but your call is important to us." The girl from Omaha wonders just how important she is. She writes him a letter, and finally, a few months later, the agent calls and sends her out on a cattle call for an infomercial. But to no avail.

And that's the last she hears from her agent. A few months later she calls and finds that the number is disconnected. Somehow, in her heart of hearts, she knew it was too good to be true.

What happened? Was the agent an absolute phony? Just one step ahead of the sheriff? Not in the legal sense. The agent did occasionally send his "clients" out on auditions, and a couple of times he actually got somebody a job. This, by definition, makes him an actors' agent. But his real business, his "star client," was the photographer. Every time he sent his friend another hopeful model or actress, he received a third of the photo fee. This is a scheme that is a legal as it is misleading and sleazy. And all our young lady can do is chalk it up to experience.

How could this young woman have avoided a costly detour on the road to fame and fortune? It's true that any prospective model or actor must have a portfolio of photographs. And that will cost money. But agents who actually get their clients jobs in the industry don't have to work as front men for photographers. They never charge fees for classes, photos, or "processing," and they receive a 10 percent or 15 percent commission only *after* the client has been paid for a job.

Before signing with any agent, ask to see his or her résumé when you hand over your own. Get a list of past and current clients and study their track records. A good drama coach may have recommendations, as will those who are actually working in the business. You can also call the Screen Actors Guild at (213) 465-4600, and for only $3 they will send out a list of reputable agents. Of course, those who are successful may not work with newcomers, but no one said it would be easy.

Another approach is to send a résumé to the film schools at USC and UCLA and volunteer as a performer in student productions. If you're chosen, you'll have a videocassette of your performance as well as a credit. And who knows? The student director just might turn out to be another Steven Spielberg!

Location Scouts Out for a Fast Buck

In cities where movies are made, there are a lot of ways to get in on the act. Those who don't yearn for the limelight may find that their property has star potential. Or so they may be told.

Most movie studios and production companies have their own location scouts. These people go out and find suitable places to shoot each and every scene in a feature film, TV show, or commercial. Some scenes are shot on studio back lots with artificial scenery and facades, but there is also a need for real houses, office buildings, and apartments.

This has created an opportunity for independent location companies to make a profit. These firms send out commission-only salespeople to knock on doors and sign up owners of "interesting" real estate. For a modest fee, say $40 to $60, owners can have their homes or properties photographed, described, and placed in a catalog. Once you're in the book, your residence may be chosen for a scene in a commercial, TV show, or even a major film. The fee for a half or whole day's shoot varies, but it's usually quite lucrative.

So what's the catch?

Some of the locations signed up by independent companies actually do end up on film. But like the actors' "agent" who makes most of his income from photo commissions, the sign-up fees are the lifeblood of these firms. Anyone who wants to get in on the lights, cameras, and action of the movie world can call a studio-related location company and sign up for free. The odds of being chosen are still slight, but at least it won't cost you anything. And as often as not, properties that aren't in anybody's catalog get spotted by a location scout just by chance.

If your home is selected, be prepared to earn your money. Having a camera crew on the premises for a day or a week is profitable and exciting, but it can also be a pain in the neck. You may have to board your Saint Bernard, put valuables in storage, and have your furniture rearranged. And your privacy will definitely be subject to invasion.

But that's showbiz. Only you can decide if it's worth it.

STUNT SCHOOLS

Jumping out windows, walking through flames, and serving as a human
punching bag may not sound like much of a way to make a living. But
to thousands of young people who aspire to be stuntmen and -women,
performing such daredevil feats is an exciting and profitable pursuit.

For those who work regularly, a career as a movie and television stuntperson can provide a generous living, opportunities for travel, and the
chance to serve as a double for some of the most celebrated talents on
screen. The occasional injuries and the almost guaranteed aches, pains,
and arthritis that accompany the job seem a reasonable price to pay for
an exhilarating career.

But breaking into the profession, as with any area of show business, is
easier said than done. At present there are only about four hundred ac-
tively employed stuntpeople, and another eight hundred who call themselves stuntpersons but work only rarely. There are several stunt
organizations, and they all have strict membership requirements. For example, in order to join the United Stuntwomen's Association, one must
be sponsored by three active members, belong to the Screen Actors Guild
(SAG), and earn at least $30,000 a year as a stuntwoman.

Clearly you can't just fly off a roof without some training, and getting
the proper credentials and preparation is a hurdle in itself. The reality is
that most stunt coordinators generally hire those whose skill and safety
records have already been established. Most stunt performers are also
members of SAG. The requirements are the same for stuntpersons as for
actors, and membership is a requirement for working on any SAG film.

From Toronto to San Diego, there are stunt schools that come and go.
Many of them are operated by failed actors who have worked only briefly
in films and who return home to cash in on other young hopefuls. Many
of them promise to get their students a SAG card, an agent, and valuable
contacts.

But most of these promises are as empty as a stage after the last curtain
falls. The prevailing operative here is money, and the owners of many of
these schools collect it as fast as they can. They may teach their appren-
tices a few tricks of the trade, but more often than not the training is dan-

gerously incomplete. As for entree to sought-after jobs, most graduates find they're on their own—and many dollars poorer.

If you would rather crash cars than sell them, remember that no one can guarantee employment. Unfortunately, there are no specific guidelines for becoming a stuntperson, and even the associations do not offer specific assistance. The best advice is to network with people in the industry, because in Hollywood it really is "who you know." If you've just gotten off the bus from Kansas and don't have a clue where to start, you might begin by working as an extra and talking to the stunt coordinator on the set, or by enrolling in an acting class and networking through your instructor and classmates. As for stunt schools, each one is different. Don't write anybody a check until you receive names of former students and talk to them personally.

Working as an Extra

Those who are waiting in the wings for that big break often seek work as movie or TV extras. Even those in other fields may decide to add a little adventure and cash to their lives by appearing occasionally as extras.

We've all read about the struggling young actress who appears in a "cast of thousands" crowd scene, is spotted by the director or leading man, and either gets discovered, makes a brilliant marriage, or both. In the land of happy endings, this too has happened.

But not very often. Most frequently, a day in the life of an extra is grueling, and it starts early (unless you get called for a night shoot, which can run from dusk to dawn). You may have to stand around in hot, cold, or wet weather, and you probably won't be granted the same perks as the regular cast and crew. Treatment varies, of course, with each production. But it's not uncommon for extras to dine on cellophane-wrapped sandwiches while a trendy caterer rolls in gourmet fare for the "real" actors.

Still, being a extra provides a chance to be in a movie, TV show, or commercial, and you get paid for your fifteen seconds of fame. Although you probably won't be hobnobbing with the stars, you may meet some interesting people. And if you aspire to bigger roles, this is a chance to put your networking skills to good use.

Just watch out for hustlers with their hands out. You don't have to train to be an extra, and you shouldn't pay any fees to register with an employment agency. SAG now registers extras, and membership is required in order to work on a SAG film. You should also be prepared for the expense of a varied wardrobe, as extras are usually asked to bring several changes of clothing to the set.

THE OLD CASTING COUCH

Everybody's heard about the casting couch routine, and you'd think that no one in this day and age would fall for it. But the practice continues, and young women who need reassurance of their attractiveness are easy targets.

Recently a "modeling agent" ran an ad in a college newspaper, seeking new clients. Like other scam artists in this milieu, his primary aim was to photograph the girls, promise them work, and collect a fee for the pictures. But unlike other phony agents who are simply after money, this slimy fellow was more than willing to take his fee out "in trade."

When Marilyn, a sophomore, answered his ad, she was given the address of a one-bedroom apartment not far from the campus. When she arrived, several other girls were sitting around the living room, waiting for their interview. One of them confided, "I know a girl who didn't have money for her photographs, but Joel [the agent] let her make it up by doing housework."

Marilyn didn't consider that a good sign and began to grow uneasy. At least there was safety in numbers. When her turn came, she was asked to walk back and forth across the bedroom while Joel appraised her assets. "Not bad. I think we can use you," he said, availing himself of the royal "we."

"What will this cost me?" Marilyn asked, wanting to get to the bottom line.

"Well, my normal fee is six hundred dollars, but if you're short of cash we can always work something out."

"Six hundred!"

"Don't you think you're worth it?" he said, taking careful aim at her fragile ego.

That stopped her. "Well—"

"You can pay me something now and maybe come over tomorrow night and cook my dinner."

Fortunately, Marilyn's self-esteem was only moderately shaky. She very much wanted the ego boost of professional validation, but she sensed that this stranger, who used his bedroom as a studio and an office, was not her ticket to fame and fortune.

But others weren't as wise. A few weeks later Marilyn saw the agent's name in the paper, and it wasn't in the entertainment section. He had been accused of assaulting a minor, and there were allegations of sexual coercion. Although no indictment resulted, it was clear that he had been using the casting couch, as it were, to enhance his love life.

Each year countless young women are lured by scam artists offering show business entree in return for money or favors. Those in need of ego bolstering are the most susceptible. The best defense is a healthy dose of self-esteem.

Ethnic Rip-Offs

The ad caught her eye immediately. She was a Latina mother, determined to become a stage mom. The small advertisement in a Spanish-language newspaper seemed to offer the break she'd been waiting for. A film was underway, and they needed Latino extras for a crowd scene. How perfect for her three beautiful muchachas! For this job they didn't even have to speak English, and each of them could earn more than $100 a day. Plus lunch!

Kids in tow, she took a bus to the agency, hoping to be first in line. There were only a few people in the reception room, and after a half-hour wait her family was escorted into a paneled office. Speaking in Spanish, the man asked if she had brought head shots. What? Pictures of her children, he answered, just their faces.

She thought of the long bus ride and wondered how and where she'd ever find a photographer who could quickly provide the necessary glossies. Fortunately she didn't have to go anywhere.

"We can take the pictures here," the man explained.

It would cost her $25 per child, but maybe she could pay the rent a little late. After all, at more than $100 a day for several days' work, it was an incredible opportunity and a chance for her kids to be discovered.

One at a time the girls were lined up against the wall and photographed. As is. No makeup, hairstyling, or special lighting. When their mother asked if she could have copies of the photos, she was told, "These are for our files."

When she and the kids trudged home, they were $75 poorer but starry-eyed. Our stage mom waited for the phone to ring ("We'll call you"), but expectant days turned into weary weeks. When she finally summoned the courage to ring the office and inquire when the movie was being filmed, she was told that her girls were "on file." Same song, different beat.

Ethnically targeted movie scams are very effective, for ads in non-English papers are quick to elicit hope and trust. Here again, the rule applies: Never pay an agent or agency for photographs.

13

Scams
on
the
Internet

The information superhighway is here! With a growing number of American households sporting personal computers, and an increasing percentage of them subscribing to on-line services, we're entering a new world of electronic communication. And along with the obvious convenience of having much of the world literally at our fingertips comes the inevitable downside.

Scam artists of all varieties, from pimple-faced hackers to international terrorists, now have access to whole new field of victims. While it can take telemarketers and direct mail scammers hours, days, or even weeks to contact thousands of potential "customers," an on-line bulletin board can provide access to large numbers of people instantly. As you can imagine, the possibilities are endless.

In this brave new frontier, the often indistinct line between what's legal and what's not is still blurry. Even when on-line legalities are more clearly defined, enforcement is challenging, to say the least. The same tools we use to protect our privacy on-line, including user IDs and electronic mail addresses, are the same tools scam artists employ to hide their identities and evade detection. At the moment, undercover "cyber rangers" are beginning to monitor bulletin boards, but the task is monumental. We all need to be aware of possible scams and be our own cops. Below are just a few of the situations to watch out for. But know that before you finish reading, a whole new set of scams will no doubt be up and running.

Parents Beware: Pedophiles On-Line

People use the Internet to fulfill inappropriate sexual fantasies. Much has been written about on-line dating and mating. In fact, some marriages have resulted from on-line "meetings," and a case may be made for "safe sex" via computer, when it involves consenting adults who prefer it to the riskiness of singles' bars.

But love letters via E-mail can range from the romantic to the truly menacing. And where there's use, there is inevitably abuse. Unfortunately, Internet surfers with unwholesome agendas haven't hesitated to "reach out and touch someone," and that person is often someone young. With today's kids becoming computer literate at such an early age, it's not unusual for three-year-olds to know how to get into a program. Pedophiles now have a virtual playground at their fingertips.

There has been at least one well-publicized incident of a middle-aged man who set up a meeting with a young girl after carrying on an X-rated on-line correspondence. Such relationships often begin in apparent innocence, with predators offering false information about their age and personal attributes. When trust and friendship have been established, they move in for the kill. Latchkey kids who are lonely and hungry for attention are prime targets for exchanges that over time become increasingly provocative. Here's how such a scenario might unfold.

Jennifer is thirteen and spends a lot of time at home alone. Her parents divorced last year, and during the week she lives with her mother who works full time. She wears braces, and her heart on her sleeve; she pines for a heartthrob who barely knows she's alive. An only child, Jennifer has strict orders to go straight home after school, do some light chores, and then start on her homework. When Jennifer's grades begin to slip, her father buys her a personal computer in hopes that it will improve her performance.

And it does. The spellcheck and thesaurus options of her word-processing program help Jennifer's compositions shine, and by subscribing to an on-line service she has unlimited access to research materials. As she develops facility on the computer, she discovers that people all over the country are "talking" to one another. For the first month or so, Jennifer just reads the messages posted by other subscribers and enjoys a vicarious thrill.

Then one day on a bulletin board she sees a message from a boy who lives in the next town. He mentions a book she's read and asks for help on a paper he's writing on the Civil War.

Our young wallflower decides to take a chance. She sends "Joe" a letter and tells him about an essay she wrote on General Lee. She doesn't really expect a reply. When "Joe" responds via E-mail within the hour, Jennifer's bleak day is suddenly brighter.

"Joe" forgets to mention the Civil War, but he writes that he's a sixteen-year-old basketball player, with dark hair and eyes, and that he's headed for college. And he wants to know all about Jennifer. What does she look like? What does she like to do for fun?

The messages are simple at first, and Jennifer takes just a bit of "creative license" as she describes herself sans braces to this neat-sounding guy. That afternoon she doesn't get much homework done. To her great surprise (surely he must have lots of girls he can write or talk to), her new pen pal writes back that he's just broken up with his girlfriend and is feeling "really lonely." It's nice, he says, to have someone he can just talk to.

Jennifer buys in big time. Now she hurries home from school with something wonderful to look forward to. This good-looking athlete seems to be interested in her. Well, at least the "her" that she exposes from the safety of her bedroom. Each day their correspondence becomes more personal, more vulnerable, and finally "Joe" confides that he's begun to fantasize about her.

This is fine with Jennifer, because her rejection at school and her parents' inattention are now countered by daydreams of her on-line "boyfriend." When he admits, rather shyly at first, that he wants to kiss her, Jennifer is thrilled. Electronically transmitted caresses are exchanged.

Pretty soon innocent kisses become passionate embraces, and before long, "Joe's" amorous reveries become more explicit. Against the backdrop of a romantic dreamscape, Jennifer's partner-in-fantasy introduces her to "what really turns a guy on."

Jennifer is both unsettled and aroused. She knows that her friend's graphic descriptions are what her parents would call X-rated, but the explicit descriptions of sexual encounters are filtered through the veil of her romantic longings. When "Joe" suggests that they exchange photos, Jennifer panics. If he sees a picture of her with wires on her teeth and without curves, she'll never hear from him again. She finally mails a snapshot of a bikini-clad older cousin to a post office box. Two days later she receives a picture of a young Adonis, signed "with love."

She's now consumed with infatuation—and guilt. She knows her mother "would kill her" if she knew about her "friend," and she feels terrible that she sent a fraudulent photo. But this is the most exciting thing ever to happen in her young life. Her furtive on-line "affair" feels at once terrifying and safe, and as the missives become increasingly crude, she rationalizes that this is "love."

Such a situation can never end happily for a child. At the very least, she'll feel hurt and betrayed. If your teenager spends hours at a computer with on-line capacity, you should pay attention. Ask about on-line activities and keep your antennae attuned for possible unsavory relationships. You may even wish to warn your kids what to watch out for, just in case.

MEDICAL FACTS AND FICTION

Betty was a young cancer patient, and like most who are diagnosed with a serious illness, she was overwhelmed with helplessness and a sense of isolation. But while recuperating from surgery, she found that her computer allowed her to access a wealth of research on her disease, as well as enabling her to communicate with others who shared her fears and concerns. The information she obtained proved helpful in her decision making, and commiserating with other patients was a great comfort.

The positive side of on-line medical bulletin boards is that you can locate clinical trials and the latest treatments in a matter of minutes. The bad news is that not all the information is valid. Experts worry that health myths and misinformation are already flooding computer networks, and it's a phenomenon that's likely to flourish.

The problem lies not with library research or information placed by professionals and legitimate organizations. Trouble brews when lay-people start exchanging unproven treatments and remedies. In Betty's case, the information she received from other cancer patients was both enlightening and sound. But all too often, on-line users share anecdotal cures for a multitude of ailments, many of which are totally unfounded. And while a homeopathic treatment for the common cold can't do much harm, those with life-threatening conditions can easily fall into a snake-oil pit filled with worthless or injurious advice.

There are laws and regulations governing claims made about herbs, vitamins, and nonprescription drugs, but at present there is no way to oversee the counsel of well-meaning folks whose on-line advice is tanta-mount to practicing medicine without a license. Ozone therapy, un-orthodox cures for AIDS, and pinhole eyeglasses that supposedly correct vision are just a few of the unconventional and unproven treatments that circulate in cyberspace.

And laypersons aren't the only ones whose advice you should be wary of. Even those with alleged credentials such as "cancer researcher" or "certified nutritionist" should be regarded with caution. Diploma mills readily hand over storebought degrees for a few hundred dollars.

So if "Doctor Daisy," with or without a title behind her name, suggests some strange concoction that cured her grandmother's arthritis, take it with a grain of salt. Better yet, don't take it at all.

14

$\mathcal{S}$ TAIRWAYS TO $\mathcal{H}$ EAVEN:

$\mathcal{R}$ ELIGIOUS AND

"$\mathcal{I}$ MMORTALITY"

$\mathcal{S}$ CAMS

The United States population includes Christians, Jews, Muslims, Buddhists, Hindus, Sikhs, Rastafarians, white witches, and more. In this land of religious freedom we have the legal right to pursue our beliefs as long as we don't infringe on the rights of others. Faith can be traditional or New Age. On today's bestseller lists are titles that report out-of-body experiences and encounters with angels. And in our troubled world we are witnessing a return to spiritual values.

All well and good. But to confirmed scam artists, nothing is sacred. The slick at heart embrace religion and spirituality with alarming enthusiasm. From televangelists who bleed their flocks to faith healers who make them pay for "miracles," these kinds of racketeers are especially heartless—and all too common.

Faith Healers

Those disillusioned with both traditional and alternative methods of healing are prime targets for phony faith healers. While many in the medical profession can testify to legitimate cases of unexplained recoveries and spontaneous remissions, many charlatans of various sorts take aim at the truly desperate.

These conjurers manipulate their audience's desire for suspended belief and use many of the same tricks as accomplished magicians. But while the latter's agenda is merely to entertain, fraudulent healers have the sinister goal of hyping the hopeless right out of their money.

The tricks are numerous and sometimes incredibly obvious. One so-called psychic surgeon appeared actually to grasp matter from inside a person's body and dramatically cast it out. These "demons" were nothing more than chicken parts, and they materialized through the same skills used in sleight-of-hand maneuvers.

In other instances, "miracle cures" are the result of the well-known placebo effect, transient remissions or paid-for "plants" in the audience who are in on the scam. And when a miracle fails to occur, the preacher heaps guilt on the recipient who "didn't have enough faith." In many cases, the damage to the not-really-healed is twofold. The victim not only pays for a worthless cure but also may delay seeking effective treatment.

Cults and Brainwashing

In November 1978, Representative Leo Ryan and others traveled from San Francisco to Guyana to investigate a cult headed by the Reverend Jim Jones. Initial interviews with cult members registered no complaints, but later, when it became clear that many of Jones's followers wanted desperately to escape, plans were made for their rescue.

But it was not to be. As they began boarding the plane that would carry them to safety, Ryan and four others were murdered in a hail of bullets. And that was just the beginning. Before the ordeal was over, more than nine hundred cult members were ordered to swallow poisoned Kool-Aid in a mass suicide/murder. The world was stunned, and "cult" became a four-letter word in the public consciousness.

Because of the Jonestown incident, and more recently the fiery deaths of the Branch Davidians in Texas, many think that cult leaders are all wild-eyed radicals, attracting only those on the lunatic fringe. What few realize is that Jim Jones initially gained prominence because of his credible efforts on behalf of the poor. Before taking his flock to Jonestown, he played a role in the San Francisco power structure, turning out crowds of followers to support various political candidates. When news of the Jonestown massacre hit the headlines, many prominent Californians reeled with shock and disbelief.

Cult leaders are by definition charismatic and, like Jones, often seem to have admirable agendas. The smoothest of them appeal not only to the less advantaged but also to an increasingly mainstream audience. Today's cults embrace business and recovery groups as well as religion or spirituality. Because the term signifies different things to different people, many members of cultlike organizations insist that they simply belong to a church or club.

But what differentiates a cult from a harmless fraternity is control. Various forms of brainwashing exist in these groups, which are estimated to number anywhere from several dozen to a few thousand throughout the United States. Once individuals enter the fold, contact with the outside world is generally discouraged. Isolation from family and friends is often accomplished through sleep and/or food deprivation, peer pressure, hours of forced indoctrination, and slected punishments. Sexual exploitation of women and children is not uncommon. There is an "us against them" mentality, with outsiders being portrayed as evil or, at best, unenlightened. And more often than not, financial contributions are expected and ultimately demanded.

Who is vulnerable to the wiles of unscrupulous leaders? Certainly those who feel alienated and unfulfilled are at special risk. Recruitment tactics are often subtle and sophisticated, offering the lure of financial success or spiritual peace. Some groups have even trained young women to use their sexual wiles to draw in new male members.

Experts say that prevention in the form of education is the best hope. But if you have a friend or relative who you think is beyond that point, you may wish to contact a specialist in the field. Those who refer to themselves as deprogrammers (a specialty that is becoming increasingly discredited) often resort to aggressive tactics that include kidnapping cult members and returning them to their families. "Exit counselors" employ a more low-key approach and do not hold individuals against their will. Those wishing further information on the subject can call the Cult Awareness Network at (312) 267-7777.

TELEVANGELISTS CRUSADE FOR CASH

No sane person would think of inviting a thief into his or her bedroom, but that's where a lot of us keep our televisions. Televangelists have racked up as much bad publicity as Mafia chieftains in recent years, yet these slick operators keep raking in the dollars.

Unfortunately, the target audience for this kind of religious hype consists mainly of the elderly, the sick, the poor, and the uneducated. Those who lack the transportation or physical ability to attend regular church services are easy marks for on-air evangelists. These proselytizers may wail about the imminence of doomsday, but time certainly seems to be on their side.

As with other TV personalities, these preachers become intimate strangers, as weekly appearances create feelings of solidarity and trust. Once insinuated into their viewers' lives, asking for money is a piece of cake. On a first-name basis with both God and their congregation, these latter-day Elmer Gantrys skillfully promote the idea of "our" church, "our" program, and of course, "our" money. They invite listeners to call in on "prayer lines," which is an effective way of expanding their mailing list for soliciting still more contributions. Televangelists often tell their flocks that without their support the broadcast will not continue. Some claim that "outsiders," in league with the devil, are out to stop them from preaching God's word.

In some cases, contributions by credit card are encouraged, but checks and plain old cash are always welcome. Guilt (for not doing enough) and gratitude (for prayers) are twin buttons used to loosen up the couch-potato cash flow.

If you are considering sending money in response to these types of pitches, you should stop in your tracks. There are many legitimate and worthwhile organizations, some religiously oriented, in need of charitable donations. You can receive more information by calling the National Charity Information Bureau at (212) 929-6300.

Cryonics: Science or Science Fiction?

For those who aren't sure there's a hereafter, there is the dubious option of preserving oneself for the not-too-distant future. Cryonic organizations now make it possible for individuals to have their bodies frozen immediately after death in hopes of being revived at some later time.

Cryonic preservation, however, is purely speculative. Although some animals have been revived after having their temperatures lowered close to the freezing point, no creature has ever survived a long-term chill at the temperature of liquid nitrogen. What we can do successfully is freeze sperm and eggs and use them years later in in-vitro fertilization procedures. And as technology continues to advance, some scientists envision the prospect of tiny "nanorobots" that can be injected into the bloodstream to repair frozen body cells.

But despite current and projected accomplishments, most physicians and medical researchers consider cryonics nothing more than a lucrative scam. Advocates accuse the medical establishment of shortsightedness at best and witch hunting at worst. Whatever one's position, this brave-new-world concept poses a number of philosophical questions: If freezing and reanimation ever were to become commonplace, what impact would the practice have on our already overpopulated world? And when one regains mortality, what about the psychological problems associated with losing loved ones and coping with an unfamiliar world?

Despite the obvious problems, more and more people are signing up for the chance at a second time around. Some are wealthy; others arrange to pay for their cold storage with life insurance policies. Whether or not cryonics falls into the category of a scam cannot be clearly determined, for who can say for sure that today's science fiction won't become tomorrow's reality? It is safe to say, however, that if you're interested in becoming a soul-on-ice, proceed with great caution and arm yourself with abundant research.

And if you'd like a shot at immortality at bargain rates, for $35 a Seattle-based company will encapsulate and preserve your genes. Unlike cryonics, no claims are made as to the possibility of reanimation. Although fragments of DNA have been recovered from millions of years past, they become compromised with age. Unlike the scientists who reconstructed T-rexes and raptors in *Jurassic Park,* real-life experts are unlikely ever to re-create an entire organism from a few specks under a microscope.

The appeal of genetic preservation, accomplished by rubbing one's finger against a piece of gauze and then sending it off in the mail with a check, is mostly an exercise in ego. This procedure allows one's unique attributes to be bottled and retained for future generations of scientists to analyze. Some might label it a scam, while others would consider it the ultimate souvenir. Not a bad gift idea for the person who has everything.

15

İNFOMERCIALS

A Seattle woman laughed when the movie came out: She had been "sleepless in Seattle" for years. She'd tried everything from hypnosis to herbs but was never able to curb her night-owl tendencies. But she learned to catnap in the afternoons and frequently mused, "I'd rather have insomnia than some ailment that costs me a fortune."

Then came middle-of-the-night infomercials. Now when the woman was shunned by the Sandman, her channel surfing invariably turned up some aging actress pitching her very own antiwrinkle cream or the latest exerciser. Responding to promises of restored youth, increased sex appeal, and get-rich-now schemes, the once-solvent insomniac found that her restlessness was becoming an expensive habit.

Are all infomercials a scam? Aren't there some good products out there? As with all sales ploys, we need to be objective and inquisitive. The special lure of infomercials is that they often assume the style of a news program or talk show to enhance their credibility. And because TV time comes cheap at three A.M., they have the advantage of a full half hour to get you to reach for your favorite credit card.

Faces "Before" and "After" — Truth or Trickery?

Unlike sixty-second commercials with paid actors, infomercials frequently use ordinary people who swear that the product of the moment has changed their life by making them younger-looking, sexier, or rich — or all three. The hosts on these programs are often movie or television personalities who moderate the show and conduct interviews like Barbara Walters or Larry King wannabes.

So what's wrong with this picture? Are all those nice fresh-faced ladies lying through their bonded teeth? Is the magic mask of the moment a worthless heap of mud, or is it, at least in part, responsible for those smooth and smiling countenances?

When beauty products are advertised, we almost always see "before" and "after" pictures. But hairstyling, makeup, and lighting all have a tremendous impact on photographs. When assessing a rejuvenated appearance, take these elements into account. But the real beauty of infomercials is that unlike still ads, they don't have to rely on photos alone. In infomercials you get to hear as well as see newly glowing faces, as women chat like girlfriends right there in your living room.

Just keep in mind that until science comes up with a truly miraculous answer to aging, beauty in a bottle can be of only marginal benefit. And those radiant faces you see on the screen are very likely attractive to begin with, glowing from an off-camera facial that temporarily provides a smoother and lifted look, and benefitting from professional tricks of the trade.

While the advertised product may well be as good as anything else on the market, it's unlikely that those pitched in the wee hours have any real edge over those developed by the well-paid staffs of major cosmetic firms. But what they may do is charge more. A *lot more!* If you see a product that interests you, such as a lotion containing gycolic or lactic acid, do some comparison shopping at both department and discount stores. See what they're charging for similar products. Often the store prices are less, and you don't have to pay for shipping or handling. Or consult your dermatologist; he or she may recommend a prescription-strength cream that costs the same or even less than store-bought solutions and may be more effective.

You-Too-Can-Get-Rich Programs

And then there are shows that interview formerly just plain folks who now spend their days idling on pristine beaches, counting their shekels. These nouveau riche never had the benefit of a Rhodes scholarship, nor do they have "any special skills." And nope, they didn't get lucky in the lottery.

What they do tell you, in such earnest tones, is that they followed the Program (memorialized in a convenient package of tapes and books) created by the show's financial wizard, who himself used to be just your standard guy. The message is simple and seductive: By working in your spare time (whatever that is), and following the Program (which costs only something-nine ninety-five), you too can soon be lolling around on the sandy white beach of your choice. Oh, it does take work, but by golly, if a one-time burger flipper can do it, so can you!

I'm not saying there isn't worthwhile advice in some mail-order cassettes. But again, be reasonable and shop around. Bookstores and libraries are filled with books offering financial advice, and local colleges and universities offer courses in real estate, investment, finance, and setting up a home-based business. It's a safe bet that the TV guru doesn't know anything that notable business and financial leaders have carelessly overlooked.

And remember that midnight marketers carefully tailor their shows to reel you in. For example, some offer their 800 number exactly 13 $\frac{1}{2}$ minutes into the program, because research shows that's when buyers are most likely to bite. And many infomercials are now broadcasting during peak viewing hours, trying to blend in with regular nonpaid programming and issuing their disclaimers in small print.

If on some occasion you feel that impulse has gotten the better of you, remember this: You must receive merchandise advertised on television within thirty days (or whatever time frame was promised) from the *moment* you recite your credit card number. If the goods don't arrive on time, and you're not informed, you are free to cancel. If you return a product (and most of them have money-back guarantees), and it still shows up on your credit card, you have sixty days to contest the billing, then your credit card company has thirty days to respond. You don't have to pay a penny until the matter is cleared up.

16

$\mathscr{S}$ INGLES

$\mathscr{S}$ CAMS

Every now and then you see a bumper sticker that proclaims HAPPINESS IS BEING SINGLE. But judging from the money spent on personal ads and dating services and at singles' bars, legions of unmarrieds are trying hard to relinquish their solitary status. In this industry that caters to the unattached, there are many legitimate services, some that are outright fraudulent, and others adrift in that murky area in between.

If you make a wrong choice in the dating game, the consequences can vary from wasting a half-hour on the phone to losing some of your hard-earned money to losing your health or life. As always, when venturing into territory that involves the heart, special caution is warranted.

$\mathcal{S}$OCIAL $\mathcal{C}$LUBS

After nearly thirty years of wedded bliss, George found himself widowed and alone. His children were grown and gone, and his few friends at work were involved with their families, just as he had once been. In his late fifties, George was a shy, quiet man who found himself uncomfortable with his needs for female companionship.

After two years of mourning, he surveyed his options. He considered himself too old for singles' bars or dating services but not yet ready to square-dance with seniors. One day while skimming through a magazine for singles, he came across a small ad for a "social" club. Members, it claimed, would be discreetly put in touch with lovely women of good character.

Because he felt awkward in social situations and didn't want to risk rejection, George decided to send in his initial processing fee and see what happened. In return for his money, he received a photograph and the address of a lovely woman. Although he wasn't much of a writer, the widower found it easier to express his thoughts on paper than to confide in a stranger face-to-face.

In response to his first missive, in which he explained that he was looking for a serious relationship, George received a promising note in the return mail. Along with another photo, the woman told him she too had lost a spouse and was seeking someone special to fill the void in her life. She encouraged George to send his membership fee to the club so they could begin a proper correspondence.

Impressed by the woman's pictures and the content of her note, George decided to take a chance. After a short time, their letters assumed an intimate tone, and soon the woman was speaking of love and offering sexual innuendos. When George offered to buy her a plane ticket so they could meet, his pen pal replied, "As soon as I take care of some financial obligations that resulted from my husband's death."

Gentleman that he was, the reserved widower offered a loan to tide her over until the estate was settled. The money was graciously accepted, and plans were tentatively made for a future visit. Finally, when George grew insistent, the woman agreed to meet him on a designated day.

Thrilled to finally be meeting this damsel of his dreams, George put a bottle of champagne on ice, purchased a dozen long-stemmed roses, and headed for the airport. When the passengers disembarked, he stood amid the crowd, searching each face that came down the ramp. When all the passengers had deplaned, George was still standing there, flowers in hand, waiting for a slender woman with long black hair.

Even when an airline official told him that no one by his woman's name had been on the flight in question, he still had hope. But when his home answering machine held no message and his phone remained quiet all evening, he began to fear the worst.

A trip to the woman's home town resulted in a futile trip to her "address," a post office box in a seedy part of town. Further checking revealed that the owner of the box was a well-heeled fellow who had been running this scam for some time.

Although I can't say that all such operations are rip-offs, it's never wise to send money to someone you've never met or don't know well. If you enter into a long-distance relationship or correspondence, through either a social club or serendipity, insist on developing, at the very least, a telephone liaison and make sure you have both home and work numbers of your heartthrob. Better yet, push for a face-to-face encounter as soon as possible, just in case your prince or princess turns out to be a toad. Or a rat.

MATCHMAKERS

After years of not-so-blissful single life, Carol decided to make a serious investment in her future. Fed up with singles' bars, personal ads, and disappointing blind dates, she heard about an exclusive introduction service that billed itself as a "marriage brokerage." For a $5,000-plus fee, this crème de la crème service promised to put her in touch with a few good men.

"We're very selective about our clients," Carol was told. Before she could become an official member of the club, she would be asked to undergo a battery of tests, including an evaluation by a psychologist and a handwriting expert. An invasion of privacy? Perhaps. But Carol was assured that such intense and thorough screening was the only way to ensure a quality clientele.

Convinced that she would soon be in rarefied company, Carol sub-mitted to the rigorous inquiries and signed over a check. Then, free of the nagging obligation to "go out and try to meet someone," she went home and waited for Prince Charming to call.

The first man to dial her number was "not quite" divorced from his second wife. Another was a man who had never been to college and ad-mitted he was "just looking for a good time."

Carol was getting ready to lodge a formal complaint when the match-making firm suddenly closed its doors, with the promise that a new of-fice would open soon. Indeed, the service did debut at a new location, halfway across the globe!

There are a number of dating and matchmaking services vying for a slice of the lucrative singles pie. Some rely on videos and questionnaires; others promise personal and carefully selected introductions. Firms that abscond with their clients' money are definitely flirting with indictments, but there are also many well-intentioned dating services that are not cap-italized well enough to go the distance. Although they try their best to fulfill clients' needs, a lot of them run out of capital and are forced to shut down.

Other services, such as video-dating clubs, satisfy some of their clients but allow others to feel like wallflowers. Photogenic individuals who come across well on camera, hold status jobs, and are the "right" age, seem to attract plenty of suitors. But those who are more ordinary-looking, not so articulate, and perhaps a bit older, often find themselves rejected. They receive few if any responses to their video interview, and when they select someone they would like to meet, that person may take a pass on meeting them. Although these types of organizations do provide the ser-vices they advertise, they don't provide equal opportunities for the less than dazzling.

Before plunking down a hefty check to a professional matchmaking service of any kind, it's wise to talk to a number of past and current mem-bers and find out exactly why they were — or were not — satisfied. And the next time Aunt Martha says she knows "such a nice" boy or girl, you might take her up on it. After all, her services are free.

SCAM!

$\mathcal{B}$EWARE OF $\mathcal{P}$RINCE $\mathcal{C}$HARMING

Elaine thought she had found the perfect man. After running through the usual assortment of dates who had drinking, job, and commitment problems, she met Russell, who seemed too good to be true. He was sensitive, caring, and interested in a serious relationship. He was a good listener as well as a compelling conversationalist and insisted on taking her to the city's finest restaurants.

Soon Elaine was telling everyone that she'd finally found a fellow who treated her like a queen. She introduced Russell to her friends and family, and they were all duly impressed with his charming manners and ready smile. And unlike so many men in her past, Elaine didn't have to worry about his intentions. In record time, Russell proposed.

Thrilled but still not quite believing she was worthy of this terrific man, Elaine began to plan for their future together. Russell encouraged her to move in with him, and before long they were a team. When Russell's American Express bill came due, bearing evidence of all those pricey meals, Elaine, being a modern woman, offered to chip in. Her true love didn't object and told her he'd never loved anyone so much.

This love affair of the century might have cost her more had Elaine not received a call from the county jail. It was Russell, calling about a "misunderstanding." It seems he had cashed some checks that had, well, resulted in his arrest. Horrified, Elaine raced downtown and posted bail. But by that time, the dominoes had begun to fall. An ex-girlfriend called, claiming that Russell owed her money, and confided to Elaine that the charmer had no fewer than three former wives.

Still, he almost succeeded in convincing Elaine that he was merely the victim of a few bad breaks. It took some stern counseling from her father and another talk with the old girlfriend to make her realize that she had indeed fallen for a charismatic sociopath.

Do you think this could never happen to you? A lot of people believe they're immune until they are actually pursued by a person for whom scams are a way of life. Psychologists use the terms "sociopath" and "psychopath" interchangeably to describe such individuals. Whichever word you choose, these are men and women who essentially lack a conscience and prey on others without the slightest sense of guilt. Sociopaths are by definition charming, and they are incredibly skilled at manipulating others. The only way to protect yourself is to be on the lookout for such traits as glibness, lack of empathy, shallow or counterfeit emotions, lying, and antisocial and manipulative behavior. And keep in mind the old axiom: If he or she seems too good to be true, he or she probably is.

If you have serious suspicions about someone you're involved with, you may want to employ the services of a private investigator. If you feel this is a heartless stratagem, consider the research you would do before making a financial investment. In a world where it's commonplace to become intimate with strangers, there's a lot more at risk than money. When in doubt, don't hesitate to protect yourself.

PERSONAL ADS

Personal ads are becoming increasingly popular. Newspapers and upscale magazines as well as publications for singles now offer classified ad space for people seeking dates, serious relationships, and marriage. Even those who once scoffed at the idea of "marketing" themselves are beginning to realize that personal ads are a way to transcend the loneliness and logistics of modern single life.

Although these ads are the ultimate form of blind dating, they allow singles a chance to screen potential dates before risking a face-to-face encounter. Letters, photographs, and telephone conversations help weed out the undesirables and give hopeful lovers an opportunity to get to know each other before investing in a night on the town. Some ad writers, however, are not above resorting to scamlike tactics to attract mates or dates. While it's considered acceptable to present oneself in a favorable light, some would-be sweethearts engage in distressing deceptions.

One young woman was delighted by the large number of responses to her personal ad. She was particularly impressed by a letter and photo sent by a tall, dark, and handsome attorney standing in the back row of a group photograph. After several phone conversations, this woman agreed to meet the deep-voiced man at a nearby coffee shop. When the moment arrived, she was in for a shock! The man who welcomed her indeed had nice-looking features, but the day of the photograph he had apparently donned a toupee and stood on a chair, for he was nearly bald and stood much closer to five feet than six. Although the woman was not repelled by his physical appearance, she was considerably put off by his deceptive tactics.

Men who seek matches through the classifieds complain that women tend to hedge, fib, and tell outright lies about their weight. "Voluptuous" women often turn out to be twenty or thirty pounds overweight, and "curvy" is sometimes a euphemism for corpulent. Smart singles read between the lines and ask direct questions about those matters they consider most important. Some magazines offer Voicemail or post office boxes to implement initial communication. The more you learn before meeting a prospective date, the better.

17
Pet Scams

Question: Why would an otherwise well-adjusted adult enter into a long-term relationship with a significant other who sleeps all day, stays out until dawn, nags, whines, and demands that every whim be instantly gratified?

Answer: If you hesitated even a moment here, you've never been a cat owner.

To many of us, dogs, cats, birds, rabbits, guinea pigs, snakes, turtles, toads, and goldfish are more than just pets; they're part of the family. And some of us get pretty daffy over our critters. One young Ivy League graduate went so far as to turn his formal dining room into a bedroom (complete with mattress) for his beloved ferret and bought the little fellow his own seat on a cross-country flight.

While most of us don't provide such elaborate accommodations for our four-legged, finned, or feathered friends, we do want the best for them. And just as there is snake oil on the shelves for humans, there are overhyped products for pets that promise everything from enhancing the "bio-availability" of food to settling the stomachs of parakeets. The FDA has cracked down on some merchandise that promises to cure actual medical disorders, claiming that such advertising is restricted to approved drugs.

But shelves abound with borderline goods, which, although they may do no harm, may delay pet owners from taking Fido promptly to the vet. Talking to a trusted veterinarian about various products is the best way to avoid rip-offs and ensure that Calvin the cat will be around for all of his nine lives.

THE "FOUND PET"

Rarely does a person of sound mind take out a newspaper ad offering unspecified amounts of cash to total strangers. But when a young couple's beloved basset hound disappeared from their backyard, they wasted no time doing just that. While their children wailed in the background for Abagail, the grieving dog owners placed an ad offering a reward in a local paper and began blanketing the streets with posters.

FEMALE BASSET, 3 YRS. OLD
LOST IN WOODSIDE AREA, KIDS BROKENHEARTED
REWARD

In no time, the phone began to ring with reported basset sightings. There were false alarms: "Does she have a black tail?" and "I think I saw her yesterday." Finally, an articulate and kind-sounding man called with good news. "Is your dog on the small side," he asked, "brown and white, with a collar?"

"Yes, a red one!"

"Then I think we've found her. My neighbors have her in their backyard, but I think they plan to keep her. They got their last dog that way."

"Can we talk to them?"

"They're not home now, but why don't you come on over? I'll get her for you, and you can just take her home."

"We really appreciate this and, you know, we're offering a reward."

"I don't want the reward money. I'm a dog lover myself, and I know how it is. My ten-year-old son lost his cocker spaniel last month. All I want to do is find him a new one. Maybe we'll go to the pound."

"Then let us at least give you something for shots—"

"Maybe $50, but that's all."

The nice man made arrangements to meet the couple at a corner near a local mall. They found him as promised, concerned and sympathetic. He got into the backseat of their car and instructed them to drive down a nearby alley. All the while he told them about his lost spaniel and his sad-eyed kid. When they approached a tree-filled backyard, he instructed the couple to slow down.

"I saw their car come in just before I left," he explained, "so we're going to have to do this fast. I'm going to grab Abagail and bring her out to the car. If she's yours, and it sounds like she is, just take off."

Because time was of the essence, he asked if he could have his $50 and instructed the couple to keep their motor running. An hour later Abagail's owners were still waiting. They got out and looked over the fence of the specified yard. No dog. They walked around to the front and knocked on the door. A pleasant woman opened the door and, when confronted, said that she knew nothing of a basset hound. They believed her. Back home, they dialed the number the stranger had given them and found it to be disconnected.

Fifty dollars poorer, Abagail's owners were still dogless, heartbroken, and a little wiser. When another young man called a few days later, claiming that his girlfriend had found an injured basset, their hopes soared, but caution prevailed. It seems the young lady had taken the dog to the vet where he was treated for minor injuries, then released. She took him home and after a week or so had become quite attached. But, said the caller, "We're moving to a condo that doesn't allow pets, and besides, if she's yours, you should have her back." He didn't ask for a reward but suggested that his girlfriend be reimbursed for her cash outlay of about $200.

The couple agreed to meet him in a parking lot. They arrived at the designated time, wondering if they had gotten lucky or if this was another scam. When they didn't see anyone fitting the description of the man on the phone, they noticed another fellow pacing the sidewalk and checking his watch. The woman got out of the car and approached him, explaining that they were waiting for someone who might have found their family pet.

"That's funny," the man said, "I was supposed to meet someone here too, but I'm a little early. He says he thinks he's found my doberman." This man, too, had been asked to bring a check or cash to cover vet and food expenses. By comparing notes the lost-dog owners realized they were being romanced by yet another scam artist.

If you lose an animal and run an ad offering a reward, screen your callers carefully. Don't hand over any money until you see your pet in the flesh. And don't get emotional; that's what scam artists are counting on.

ALLEY CATS DISGUISED AS ARISTOCRATS

For many animal lovers, an adorable mutt or cuddly alley cat makes the perfect pet. But for those a bit more concerned with status, pedigreed kittens and puppies are well worth the price. Unfortunately, good breeding isn't always easy to detect.

One man learned the hard way when he responded to an ad offering Burmese kittens. A woman with a cultured voice answered the phone and volunteered to come by later that day with two little ones in tow. When she arrived, the man was impressed by her upper-crust British accent and manners. The kittens, of course, were irresistible.

Because he desired only one pet, the man had to choose between the furry siblings. As the woman described their care and feeding (baby food and designer water), he was impressed by her knowledge and expertise. Like the kittens, she seemed quite the aristocrat.

After choosing the smaller of the two cats, the man paid the woman in cash, and she promised to mail the kitten's papers the next day. It was a quick transaction and a pleasant one. But when the owner took Prince to the vet the next day for shots and a checkup, he learned that his male Burmese was in fact a cute little female street cat.

He of course called the seller immediately, but the high-toned Brit couldn't be reached. Her number was "no longer in service." But all was not lost. The kitten, renamed Princess, had no complaints. Alley cat or not, she behaved as if to the manor born and insisted on nothing less than royal treatment from her reluctant but caring owner.

Pet Cemeteries

Anyone who has loved and lost a pet knows how deeply animals can affect us. When a pet dies, some owners are content with a backyard burial, while others leave Fido or Snowball in the hands of their veterinarian. But for some, the grieving process is so intense that they feel the need to make a final and elaborate gesture.

Pet cemeteries rival human ones in every way, although their clientele is considerably more diverse. These burial grounds offer a final resting place for every kind of animal from blue-ribbon horses to the occasional pet mouse who is laid to rest in a matchbox. Some graves even sport headstones, and many are adorned with flowers. Final rites may include the reading of a poem over a pet's grave or an elaborate funeral complete with speakers and organ music.

Other services may include the sprinkling of a pet's ashes over the ocean or a wooded area, and some cemeteries send annual cards to pet owners, relaying greetings from doggie heaven. While these rites may seem like a perfect example of a rip-off to those who've never bonded with an animal, they provide a genuine service to animal lovers who need a traditional way of dealing with their grief.

While most of pet cemeteries, like their human counterparts, operate in a legal and dignified fashion, there have been cases of reported abuse. In some instances, pet carcasses have turned up in communal graves, and others have been subjected to mass cremations.

If you decide to honor your pet with a royal send-off, you may want to check out the cemetery with your local Better Business Bureau or call the district attorney's office to see if there are any complaints or indictments on record. And be alert for high-pressure salespeople who are trained to wring extra dollars from the wallets of the bereaved. Fido, wherever he's resting in peace, surely knows that your love can't be measured in dollars.

APPENDIX:
CONSUMER PROTECTION NUMBERS

ADOPTION ISSUES
National Adoption Center
1500 Walnut Street, Suite 701
Philadelphia, PA 19102
215-735-9988

National Adoption Information
Clearinghouse
11426 Rockville Pike, Suite 410
Rockville, MD 20852
301-231-6512

AUTOMOTIVE
Center for Auto Safety
2001 S. Street NW, Suite 410
Washington, DC 20009
202-328-7700

U.S. Department of
Transportation
National Highway Traffic Safety
Administration
Consumer Affairs Division
400 7th Street SW (NOA-42)
Washington, DC 20590
202-366-0123

U.S. Environmental
Protection Agency
Office of Mobile Sources
Field Operations and Support
Division
501 3rd Street NW
Washington, DC 20460
202-233-9000

CHARITABLE ORGANIZATIONS
Council of Better Business
Bureaus, Inc.
Philanthropic Advisory
Service
4200 Wilson Boulevard, Suite 800
Arlington, VA 22203
703-276-0100

CHILDREN'S ISSUES
Children's Defense Fund
25 E Street NW
Washington, DC 20001
202-628-8787

CONSTRUCTION AND REAL ESTATE
National Homeowners
Association
14150-A Willard Road, Suite 200
Chantilly, VA 22021
703-803-3400

U.S. Department of Housing and
Urban Development
Office of Public Affairs
451 7th Street SW, Room 10226
Washington, DC 20410
202-708-3161

CREDIT AND PERSONAL FINANCE
Bankcard Holders of America
6862 Elm Street, Suite 300
McLean, VA 22101
703-917-9805

U.S. Department of the
Treasury
Consumer Affairs Office
Main Treasury Building,
Room 4404
1500 Pennsylvania Avenue NW
Washington, DC 20220
202-727-7000

EDUCATION
National PTA–National Congress
of Parents and Teachers
300 N. Wabash Street, Suite 2100
Chicago, IL 60611
312-670-6782

EMPLOYMENT
Equal Employment Opportunity
Commission
1801 L Street NW
Washington, DC 20507
202-663-4900

National Association of Older
Worker Employment
c/o National Council on Aging
409 3rd Street SW, Suite 200
Washington, DC 20024
202-479-1200

National Safe Workplace
Institute
3008 Bishops Ridge
Monroe, NC 28110
704-289-6061

Screen Actors Guild
5757 Wilshire Boulevard
Los Angeles, CA 90036
213-549-6400

U.S. Department of Labor
Coordinator of
Consumer Affairs
200 Constitution Avenue NW
Washington, DC 20210
202-219-7316

ENVIRONMENTAL ISSUES
Citizens for a Better
Environment
407 S. Dearborn Street,
Suite 1775
Chicago, IL 60605
312-939-1530

Environmental Protection
Agency
Office of the Inspector
General
501 3rd Street NW 6406J
Mail Code A-109
Washington, DC 20460
202-260-4977

FOOD AND DRUGS
Consumer Health Information
Corporation
8300 Greensboro Drive,
Suite 1220
McLean, VA 22102
703-734-0650

Council on Family Health
225 Park Avenue South, 17th Floor
New York, NY 10003
212-598-3617

U.S. Department of Agriculture
Food and Consumer Services
Office of the Consumer
Service
3101 Park Center Drive
Alexandria, VA 22302
703-305-2281

GENERAL CONSUMER ADVOCACY
Center for Study of
Responsive Law
PO Box 19367
Washington, DC 20036
202-387-8030

Consumer Information Center
18 F Street NW, Room G-142
Washington, DC 20405
202-501-1794

Consumers Union of the
United States
101 Truman Avenue
Yonkers, NY 10703
914-378-2000

Public Citizen
2000 P Street NW, Suite 700
PO Box 19404
Washington, DC 20036
202-833-3000

HEALTH AND FITNESS

Aerobics and Fitness
Foundation of America
15250 Ventura Boulevard,
Suite 310
Sherman Oaks, CA 91403
818-905-0040

AIDS Clinical Trials Group
c/o National Institute of
Health
6003 Executive Boulevard,
Room 2A07
Bethesda, MD 20892
301-496-8210

American Society of Plastic
and Reconstructive
Surgeons
444 E. Algonquin Road
Arlington Heights, IL 60005
847-228-9900

U.S. Department of Health and
Human Services
Centers for Disease Control and
Prevention
Office of Public Affairs
Building 1, Room 2047
1600 Clifton Road NE
Atlanta, GA 30333
404-639-3286

INSURANCE

Consumer Insurance Interest
Group
400 N. Washington Street
Alexandria, VA 22314
703-836-9340

LEGAL ISSUES

The Information Center, Inc.
15100 Northline Road, Suite 175
Southgate, MI 48195
313-282-7171

National Consumer Law
Center
11 Beacon Street
Boston, MA 02108
617-523-8010

MEDIA ISSUES

Children's Advertising
Review Unit
c/o Council of Better Business
Bureaus
845 3rd Avenue
New York, NY 10022
212-705-0124

Federal Communications
Commission
Consumer Assistance Branch
1919 M Street NW, Room 254
Washington, DC 20554
202-632-7000

National Association for
Better Broadcasting
7918 Naylor Avenue
Los Angeles, CA 90045
213-641-4903

PRODUCT SAFETY
Consumer Protection
Agency/Nonprofit Foundation
9025 Wilshire Boulevard,
Suite 309
Beverly Hills, CA 90211
213-487-7000

U.S. Consumer Product
Safety Commission
Office of Information and
Public Affairs
Washington, DC 20207
301-504-0580

RELIGIOUS CONCERNS
Cult Awareness Network
2421 W. Pratt Boulevard,
Suite 1173
Chicago, IL 60645
312-267-7777

Free Minds
PO Box 3818
Manhattan Beach, CA 90266
310-545-7831

RETAIL AND COMMERCIAL CONCERNS
Alliance Against Fraud
in Telemarketing
815 15th Street NW 928N
Washington, DC 20005
202-639-8140

Consumers Education and
Protection Association
International
6048 Ogontz Avenue
Philadelphia, PA 19141
215-424-1441

Small Business
Administration
Office of Consumer
Affairs
409 3rd Street SW
Washington, DC 20416
202-205-6236

TRAVEL AND TRANSPORTATION
American Society of
Travel Agents
1101 King Street
Alexandria, VA 22314
703-739-2782

National Association of Transit
Consumer Organizations
11 Kellogg Boulevard East,
Suite 1501
St. Paul, MN 55102
612-227-5171

UTILITIES
Organization for Consumer Justice
11117 Nursery Road
Hagerstown, MD 21740
301-582-1766